Cathlene Williams
Association of Fundraising Professionals

Lilya Wagner
The Center on Philanthropy at Indiana University

COEDITORS-IN-CHIEF

EXPANDING THE ROLE OF PHILANTHROPY IN HEALTH CARE

William C. McGinly
Association for Healthcare Philanthropy

Kathy Renzetti
Association for Healthcare Philanthropy

EDITORS

T0340166

JOSSEY-BASS™
An Imprint of
🟎WILEY

Number 49
Fall 2005

EXPANDING THE ROLE OF PHILANTHROPY IN HEALTH CARE
William C. McGinly, Kathy Renzetti (eds.)
New Directions for Philanthropic Fundraising, No. 49, Fall 2005
Cathlene Williams, Lilya Wagner, Coeditors-in-Chief

NEW DIRECTIONS FOR PHILANTHROPIC FUNDRAISING (print ISSN 1072-172X; online
ISSN 1542-7846) is indexed in Higher Education Abstracts and Philanthropic Index.

Microfilm copies of issues and articles are available in 16 mm and 35 mm, as well as
microfiche in 105 mm, through University Microfilms Inc., 300 North Zeeb Road,
Ann Arbor, Michigan 48106-1346.

NEW DIRECTIONS FOR PHILANTHROPIC FUNDRAISING is part of the Jossey-Bass
Nonprofit and Public Management Series and is published quarterly by Wiley
Subscription Services, Inc., A Wiley Company, at Jossey-Bass, 989 Market Street,
San Francisco, California 94103-1741.

SUBSCRIPTIONS cost $109.00 for individuals and $228.00 for institutions, agencies,
and libraries. Prices subject to change. Refer to the order form at the back of this
issue.

EDITORIAL CORRESPONDENCE should be sent to Lilya Wagner, The Center on Philanthropy at Indiana University, 550 West North Street, Suite 301, Indianapolis, IN
46202-3162, or to Cathlene Williams, Association of Fundraising Professionals,
1101 King Street, Suite 700, Alexandria, VA 22314.

www.josseybass.com

Contents

Editors' Notes

WITH HEALTH CARE PROVIDERS throughout the world facing what seem to be insurmountable challenges in providing access to quality health care, health care philanthropy is becoming ever more essential, crucial, and central to the health care enterprise.

This volume addresses some of the major issues surrounding health care philanthropy. Positioning the contribution of fundraising and relating it to the financial support for and stewardship of the health care provider will go a long way in establishing consistent policies in various parts of the world for health care delivery.

Clearly, where the philanthropic engine thrives, the crucial role of the chief executive officer, physicians, nurses, and other health care givers is more attractive and essential than ever. Here we examine the topic of measuring our performance in these areas and developing a sophisticated, professional approach in order to enhance health care philanthropy.

The chapter authors are some of the most accomplished experts working in health care philanthropy. As you will see from the essential topics that they address, it is imperative that health care development professionals understand the environment within which health care providers operate today. This understanding is essential in order to build effective philanthropy.

It is our pleasure as the editors to have brought this volume to life; at the same time, we acknowledge the dedication and commitment of the chapter authors. We welcome your attention to their perspectives based on their experience, training, and education, and

NEW DIRECTIONS FOR PHILANTHROPIC FUNDRAISING, NO. 49, FALL 2005 © WILEY PERIODICALS, INC.

we hope that their efforts will also prompt a lively discussion of the elements essential to health care philanthropy.

William C. McGinly
Kathy Renzetti
Editors

WILLIAM C. MCGINLY *is president and chief executive officer for the Association for Healthcare Philanthropy in Falls Church, Virginia.*

KATHY RENZETTI *is director of membership and communications for the Association for Healthcare Philanthropy in Falls Church, Virginia.*

Discover the key issues affecting the nonprofit health care organization as it integrates philanthropy into its strategic plan.

1

Maximizing fundraising's strategic contribution

Stephen C. Falk

"THE PRESENCE OF PHILANTHROPY is an admission that the business plan is flawed," pontificated one CEO I encountered. He was not being difficult, but truly felt relying on an abstraction such as the goodwill of humanity to fund the ongoing operations of his institution was flawed at best. Another CEO stated to me on one occasion that he truly needed philanthropy so he could raise enough money "to sandblast the administration building." Would donors find this a compelling case for philanthropy? They both have a common thread, however. Quite simply, what are realistic expectations from a mature or maturing philanthropy program, and how are these expectations negotiated? Is it enough to justify a case statement inclusion because we can raise funds around an opportunity, or does that become the proverbial "gift that eats" from the operations perspective? A former chief operating officer of a major hospital expressed her extreme displeasure with philanthropy by telling me that each time we declared a successful gift, it cost her operations dollars.

NEW DIRECTIONS FOR PHILANTHROPIC FUNDRAISING, NO. 49, FALL 2005 © WILEY PERIODICALS, INC.

"Association Healthcare Philanthropology"

The last word in the subhead above is not a typographical error; indeed it was on the hotel monitor in Kansas City, Missouri, on April 25, 2004, at a regional conference. I took a picture of it, and it sits on my desk. I believe "Philanthropology" is similar to anthropology in the mind and eye of the staff who posted the conference agenda. "Philanthropology" must be the evolution and study of donors. This may not be a bad term to consider after all. I am always amazed at the misconceptions some have about philanthropy, whether in Kansas City or anywhere else. Regrettably, it is often leadership that thinks that if they wish hard enough, their vision of philanthropy will become reality. We are in a relationship business, plain and simple. And yet when I visit with many colleagues and in my professional experience, we can all describe philanthropy offices physically distant from the campus and philosophically distant from the leadership of the organization.

One friend recently called and told me her board and CEO wanted a campaign for a "large number" as soon as possible. "No need for a feasibility study; the potential is endless," they assured her. There was only one condition: she could not solicit trustees! The vision for philanthropy was there, but the access to persons of influence and affluence was being denied. What are the chances of success in that environment?

People do not give to strangers; they give to friends, acquaintances, and colleagues. They give for a variety of reasons to those who share a vision and resources (leadership and funds). A similar misconception is that by hiring some silver-tongued fundraiser from afar, your woes will be solved. The concept of integrating the foundation leadership and staff into the hierarchy and culture of the hospital seems foreign. That fundraisers can achieve their goal on the merits of their own verbal skills and, in the case cited above, from strangers is a myth. Nothing could be further from the truth.

The fundraisers' perspective

Within our shop, we have many adages to keep us focused and humble. Among my favorites are, "Philanthropy isn't a job, it's a lifestyle," and "It is not about me." One of my mentors, who recently passed away, had an adage that has influenced me for my entire career: "If you get the credit, you are not doing your job. If you need the credit, you are in the wrong job." It is our collective task to help define philanthropy prospects, goals, and reality. What is considered to be real and valued from the vantage of the CEO, the operations vice president, and the donor must take precedence over the fundraiser's desire for a "big number." Likewise, what may be the burning passion of the administration may not be fundable through philanthropy.

If you build it, they may not come

The starting point for this "negotiation" (the balance between need, want, and feasibility) is your comprehension of the hospital's strategic plan. In August 2002, I attended, with my campaign cochair, the Association for Healthcare Philanthropy (AHP) Trustee Leadership and Philanthropy Forum in San Francisco. Bill McGinly, AHP president and chief executive officer, was conducting the session and asked the trustees if they knew the strategic goals of their respective hospital or systems. With great pride, my chair raised her hand and accurately defined our two primary strategic goals as Best Patient Experience and Best People. To my pride initially, and later to my astonishment, not one other trustee spoke. Not one trustee that day in attendance knew, or at least was willing to voice, the strategic goals of their respective institution.

I like to think of the strategic plan of the hospital as the menu from which we can order. At any given time we are highly selective, but the parameters are clearly defined. The strategic plan reflects leadership's vision and should be embedded in our vocabulary.

During our last senior management retreat, I asked each of my colleagues to consider how the foundation could provide a value-add in each component of the strategic plan. The silence was deafening. I thought I was placing the solution to selected problems on the table, but I was greeted with blank stares. Later, one of my colleagues said to me that philanthropy was problematic since it could not be guaranteed.

And therein lies an additional premise underlying the process of philanthropy negotiation. After setting expectations from the strategic plan and avoiding the gift that costs operational money to accept ("a gift that eats"), focus wherever possible on the "value-add" component. Realize that you cannot, and probably should not, guarantee that philanthropy can be secured to sandblast the building. What you can do, however, is provide the incentive and resources to complement the approved strategic plan and take your institution's mission and stature to the next level. This is one of the most compelling and rewarding dimensions of health care philanthropy: the ability to provide a benefit to those you do not know but who are in need. The health care case for support and fundraising opportunities is far more compelling than in other dimensions of philanthropy. Stated simply, health care philanthropy can save lives.

However, just because it is contained within the hospital strategic plan does not mean it is a fundable philanthropy priority. It may be worthy and it may be noble, but it may be without a donor for a long time, perhaps forever. How do we discover the common ground of meeting institutional need and philanthropy reality? Is the answer contained within the philanthropic strategic plan?

Adopting modified corporate culture to achieve corporate credibility

Philanthropy strategic planning is the double-edged sword: you must identify, cultivate, solicit, and steward, at the same time that you plan how to identify, cultivate, solicit, and steward through your strategic plan. I have known many colleagues to fall at each extreme.

There are those who simply ask. And there are those who simply plan. But neither represents the proper balance. A strategic plan for philanthropy must be balanced and complement and integrate into the corporate culture and strategic plan.

Many people contend we are professionals in the *nonprofit* environment. I think a more appropriate characterization is that we exist in a *nonprofit corporate* environment. Inherent in that assumption are business, management, and strategic planning protocols we may not normally see in a traditional nonprofit climate. Consider the strategic plan. At Northwestern Memorial Foundation (NMF), we have a comprehensive strategic plan that links directly to the parent corporation's plan. We are the child; the corporation is the parent. That is a tough concept for some. Start with the mission.

Remember the trustee who knew the strategic objectives for the hospital? All trustees need to know the mission for the foundation as well. Our mission statement is as follows (I doubt whether yours would be much different):

I. Northwestern Memorial Foundation Attracts Extraordinary Philanthropic Resources by Matching the Generous Intent of Donors with the Needs of Northwestern Memorial Hospital and Its Affiliates

II. Northwestern Memorial Foundation Serves Donors Through Personal Relationships and Consistent Communication

III. Northwestern Memorial Foundation Provides Exemplary Stewardship of Donor and Foundation Resources

IV. Northwestern Memorial Foundation Provides Substantial Support to Northwestern Memorial Hospital's Role as One of the Leading Academic Medical Centers in the United States by Investing in Patient Care, Research, Education and Community Service Missions

The mission is quite clear and concise. Moreover, it supports the parent corporation's mission of Best Patient Experience and Best People. We identify prospects and solicit gifts to benefit the hospital. We do so through relationship management and stewardship in support of the hospital. To accomplish this mission, we need partners. These partners are our colleagues at every level of the hospital structure. From the patient transport partner to the president of the hospital, each must accept the mission statement of the foundation as their personal role and challenge. Remember the adage, "Philanthropy isn't a job, it's a lifestyle." A fundraiser cannot undo a negative donor experience in the emergency room at 2:00 A.M. with a winning smile and a slap on the back. We need responsive and engaged partners at every level.

Supporting the NMF mission statement are goals (and to achieve each goal, there are objectives) to facilitate the outcome. As you can tell, without proper time management, you can be a full-time fundraising bureaucrat managing the strategic plan and not raising money. The objectives are as follows:

1. *Maximize* Fund Raising in Support of Northwestern Memorial Hospital Mission and Strategy
2. *Distinguish* Northwestern Memorial Hospital Clinical, Research, Education and Community Service Programs through strategic grant making
3. *Ensure* Exemplary Stewardship and Financial Management of NMF Assets
4. *Maintain* Strong Infrastructure Assuring Appropriate Governance, Management and Ethical Conduct

Note the first word of each objective. We maximize, distinguish, ensure, and maintain. This is powerful and direct.

Philanthropy lends itself to adaptable practice from the business world, and we should comply wherever possible with business protocol to achieve our objectives. There are several core examples from within the corporate world, and yet we often neglect even the most rudimentary. Here are a few of the important ones.

Punctuality

It seems trivial, but to arrive late for a meeting is basically telling the hosts that your time is more valuable than their own. Our rule of thumb is that we are to arrive a minimum of five minutes before the meeting begins. Work starts each day at the same time in these corporate environments. The same holds true for all donor interactions.

Communication

Communication is critical, we would all agree. As the old adage goes, tell them what you are going to say, say it, and then tell them what you just said. If you do this, there will still be a certain segment that does not quite hear the message, for whatever reason. We have taken this a step further. We provide briefing packets to our colleagues three times to reinforce the message and purpose of events. This information packet is delivered four weeks, two weeks, and, finally, one week in advance of any event. We call this process 4–2–1. Since implementing this procedure three years ago, we have never had a colleague volunteer or donor indicate he or she was not properly informed or prepared for an event. This is now part of our corporate culture, and it works most effectively.

GANTT charts

The GANTT is a long-tested business planning tool, which defines and charts all the necessary interactions to complete a project. Check with anyone in your planning office or construction office, and this person's walls will be covered with GANTT charts. We use these project plans for all events and interactions. The GANTT can be provided to anyone making inquiry as to the status of an activity. In fact, we are so integrated into this corporate planning tool and its structure that all we discuss in meetings is if someone is "off GANTT." This means that if you want to know what is going on, read the GANTT. This technique eliminates the tedium of activity reports and allows everyone to more effectively use their time.

Customer and donor friendly

Is your foundation customer and donor friendly? We define *customer* from a broad perspective. Certainly donors are customers, but so are all employees of NMH and NMF. "The measure of a man is how he treats someone who can do nothing for him" is another one of our foundation adages. Treat every stranger as a customer. A person who walks through the hospital doors is your customer. Does the hospital staff feel the same customer support toward you?

A trustee at one institution questioned a professional presentation relating to research and education. "You only forgot one thing: there was no mention of the donor in the entire document." Indeed, it was a stellar academic piece of work, but it neglected to address the source of the funds. When it was restructured, there were seventy-three references to "donor-restricted funds." The first version had none.

Do not promise more than you can deliver to the customer

My executive assistant, Virginia, has a wonderful daughter named Jessica. One day they were looking at cats for sale, and Jessica fell in love: "Mom, it is only $100, and we can take it home." Now, Virginia is very smart: she told Jessica that God would have to provide the $100 because it was "not in the budget." The next day as they walked home, Jessica reached down and picked up a $100 bill from the sidewalk!

Be careful what you promise, because you might have to deliver. I tend to be an understater of fundraising expectations. In my entire career, I have never had a physician complain when I delivered more money than I promised. But on those occasions (rare, I hope) where my enthusiasm outstripped the philanthropy I delivered, there was powerful disappointment.

Financial reporting

Is there any area of philanthropy that has more room for misinterpretation than financial reporting? It should be the most concrete of our philanthropy disciplines, and it remains one of the most difficult to dissect. If you think we are confused, how do you think the finance office and volunteers feel? We all understand Generally Accepted Accounting Principles (GAAP), and that is the one language in common with the finance office.

GAAP, however, does not capture the spirit or intent of philanthropy. A donor pledges $10 million—a combination of cash and an irrevocable estate commitment. To the donor, this is a pinnacle commitment, a transformational gift to your program. And yet the finance office sees only $5 million and questions the structure of the gift.

We are all aware of philanthropy shops that like to offer generous recognition to inflate their totals. Do you count life insurance at face value? Do you recognize National Institutes of Health funding in your totals? Do you count bequests without documentation and regardless of age? Do you book pledges without signed documentation? Regrettably, in each example cited, I am aware of prominent members of health care philanthropy and higher education communities that use each of these techniques and others to inflate their totals. Philanthropy professional credibility wanes with each example cited.

Meet with your finance staff. Never attempt to influence a GAAP number. Communicate frequently and in detail as to how you are accounting for your campaign total. Reasonable people disagree, but they should do so honorably. Treat your finance colleagues as a resource and a partner, not the adversary they often become. There is room for improvement and education on both sides of the equation.

Plan for the future

Recently the head of a major consulting firm told me the average tenure of a fundraiser was thirty-three months and declining. In business, long-term employees are valued. As members of nonprofit corporations, we should consider commitment to be a hallmark of our service. If you enter a job planning to be involved for a short period of time, you undoubtedly will make decisions like a short timer. How do we earn the respect and credibility of our corporate partners if we plan exclusively for ourselves?

Commitment changes your perspective. Are you committed? Are you committed to the profession as well as your current employer?

Right about now you are probably asking whether the employer is committed to you. You should have asked that question when you assessed the opportunity, not after you arrived. There are institutions that are revolving doors. Those are not the types of places where I seek to work, but you must evaluate that before you accept the position. Commitment is a treasured corporate value, and it must be generalized to our profession.

Conclusion

Health care philanthropy saves lives, and encouraging that philanthropy is an honorable profession. Our obligation is to the donors and the nonprofit corporations that employ us. We must adopt a modified corporate culture that enables us to convey our message and accomplish our professional objectives with integrity and to assist in the advancement of the institutions we serve. We do indeed maximize, distinguish, ensure, and maintain the relationships we develop, to ensure and optimize our institutional mission. Philanthropy is truly a lifestyle, not a job, and we should live it to the fullest so the patients, donors, staff, and the institutions we serve achieve their greatest potential.

Integration of the institutional strategic plan with our foundation volunteers, staff, and donor community is essential to achieve this optimization. This means adding value wherever possible to the mission, while recognizing that not every component of the strategic plan is fundable through philanthropy. Great medical institutions have several things in common. Foremost is superb medical care from physicians and nurses, complemented by strong collegial administrative management and outstanding research. Institutional quality will also attract philanthropy as a hallmark of distinction. Philanthropy does not symbolize the "failure of the business plan"; on the contrary, it demonstrates the faith society places in your institution and the willingness of the donor community to affirm your mission. If you build quality, patients and philanthropy will follow. You may just be as good as you say you are.

STEPHEN C. FALK *is vice president, philanthropy, at Northwestern Memorial Foundation in Chicago.*

It is not uncommon to hear of differences between the development office and the hospital's finance department. Differences arise due to different goals, audiences, needs, and measurement tools.

2

Integrating fundraising into finance

Nick G. Costa

THE MOST EFFECTIVE fundraising programs often are the result of a mission-driven organization that involves key stakeholders (including physicians, executive staff, board members, and donors) in identifying, prioritizing, and funding its needs on both a short-term and long-term basis. Short-term needs are best defined through the annual budgeting process (both operating and capital needs), while the organization's long-term aspirations may emerge from a strategic planning process.

It is not uncommon, however, to hear of differences between the development office or foundation and the hospital's finance department, despite the fact that both are responsible for ensuring the financial resources required to sustain and improve the organization's success. Differences between development and finance often are due to different goals, audiences, needs, and messages, as well as measurement tools and external pressures unique to each field.

Portions of Statement of Financial Accounting Standards No. 117, *Financial Statements of Not-for-Profit Organizations*, copyright by the Financial Accounting Standards Board, 401 Merritt 7, PO Box 5116, Norwalk, CT 06856, are reprinted with permission. Complete copies of this document are available from the FASB.

This chapter seeks to increase understanding of the goals and pressures that each area faces; it then presents a process and supporting strategies for integrating fundraising into financial needs that are consistent with the hospital's vision and mission.

Pressures on finance

Many hospitals are experiencing financial stress caused by a number of circumstances.

Deteriorating bottom line

The *New York Times* (Abelson, 2002) reported that in a little more than two years, Moody's Investor Services downgraded more than 120 nonprofit hospitals, resulting in 9 percent of Moody's nonprofit hospital portfolio considered below investment grade. The median hospital operating margin fell from 3.6 percent in 1997 to 1.7 percent in 2002. Compounding the problem of smaller operating margins are lower returns from investments and endowments seen in recent years.

Aging facilities and rapidly changing technology

Health care think tanks such as the Advisory Board (2003, p. 2) have used American Hospital Association statistics to show that demand for care is increasing at a time when "hospital facilities [are] currently at their oldest in almost a decade." Based on current and projected construction, the Advisory Board states that hospitals will need to generate an operating margin of 4.5 percent from operations and investments to update their facilities to meet market demands. "The average hospital's surplus operating revenue is simply inadequate to cover the capital investment necessary," the Advisory Board (p. 4) concludes.

Increased costs, lower payments

Hospitals are confronted with severe shortages in nurses and other professionals that are pushing up salaries, while government and private insurance programs are struggling to contain reimbursement payments at or below the rate of inflation. Dramatically higher malpractice premiums, the cost of fuel, and other operating expenses have forced some physicians' offices and hospitals to close their doors.

Reporting standards

The Enron scandal, the collapse of Allegheny Health System in Pennsylvania, and other scandals in the corporate sector have resulted in closer scrutiny and more detailed accounting and disclosures.

Pressures on development

The development office has similar pressures.

Demand for greater accountability by donors and regulators

Surveys by INDEPENDENT SECTOR and other organizations point out that donors are concerned about how well charities use their donations as they intended, particularly after the terrorist attacks of September 11, 2001 (INDEPENDENT SECTOR, 2002). Decreasing public confidence has reinforced the commitment of regulators and watchdog groups that demand that charities not only fulfill their commitments to donors, but also provide a more public accounting on the use and results of these gifts, as well as their efficiency in fundraising (see also Chapter Six, this volume).

Multiple, sometimes conflicting demands for use of donations

Decreasing bottom lines have prompted some hospitals to require fundraising for more unrestricted gifts, which is often harder to raise, while continuing to expect large gifts to support program and capital needs. Worthwhile programs such as planned giving, which provide a future benefit to charity, are postponed, and sometimes criticized, due to the short-term pressures for cash.

Difficult-to-understand reporting standards

While financial reports must be prepared using standards established by the Financial Accounting Standards Board (FASB), these reports often are difficult for donors and board members to understand when trying to assess what was raised and what gifts are pending. Not only is giving information fragmented (it is classified, dissected, and reported on multiple lines and pages of the financial statements), but fundraising activities such as grants do not appear until expenditures are made. The excitement and impact of a $500,000 grant paid over five years, for example, may take months before it is seen on the financial report. While standard accounting reports meet key hospital accounting needs, it is difficult for them alone to measure progress and growth in a development program. Surprisingly some chief financial officers are uncomfortable allowing their chief development officers (CDOs) to present reports targeted to fundraising performance to their board members.

More competition

Development programs face increasing competition today as donors have more choices where to give. Internal Revenue Service data recorded approximately 800,000 charities in 2000, almost double the number a decade ago.

Making the case for development

Pressures to maintain and increase the bottom line have prompted many health organizations to demand that all departments, including the development office, continually justify their expenses. Development officers are forced to learn, measure, and present their performances with a myriad of new metrics (see Chapter Ten, this volume). The case for development is often best made by focusing health care executives and board members on the central role of the development office: supporting and enhancing the organization's vision and mission. A development office budget of $2 million per year may be more readily understood in the context of raising $10 million annually toward the hospital's $25 million capital budget or to offset a portion of the $100 million strategic plan to modernize its campuses.

Another approach is to analyze the benchmark comparisons already used by the organization and then incorporate comparative data for development. If the organization compiles and graphs total revenue per full-time equivalent employee, for example, justification for the existing development budget (or adding to it) may be made by adding comparable performance data for development activities (see Exhibit 2.1).

Exhibit 2.1. Using a standard hospital report to make the case for development
The Finance Department of ABC Hospital prepared the following dashboard report for its executive staff and board to monitor the organization's performance. Four key indicators (Operating Margin, % Operating Margin, Revenue/Employee, and Margin/Employee) are reviewed quarterly and annually to determine progress toward efficiency.

Performance Indicators (FY 2005)

	ABC Hospital
Number of Beds	350
Occupied Beds	280
Operating Revenue	$310,000,000
Operating Margin	$5,270,000
% Operating Margin	1.7%
Margin/Occupied Bed	$18,821
Number of Employees (FTE)	2,320
Revenue/Employee	$133,621
Margin/Employee	$2,272

By adding comparative data for the foundation to this standard report, the case for both current development operations and increasing staff in the future can easily be made.

Performance Indicators (FY 2005)

	ABC Hospital	ABC Hospital Foundation
Number of Beds	350	
Occupied Beds	280	
Operating Revenue	$310,000,000	$3,750,000
Operating Expense	$304,730,000	$750,000
Operating Margin	$5,270,000	$3,000,000
% Operating Margin	1.7%	80%
Margin/Occupied Bed	$18,821	$10,714
Number of Employees (FTE)	2,320	5
Revenue/Employee	$133,621	$750,000
Margin/Employee	$2,272	$600,000

Note: "Operating Margin" for ABC Hospital Foundation represents funds available after foundation expenses for hospital operations, capital or program needs, and endowments.

Among the points worth highlighting in Exhibit 2.1 are that ABC Foundation has significantly high returns, despite a markedly smaller number of employees, in such key areas as Operating Margin, % Operating Margin, Revenue/Employee, and Margin/Employee. If the organization's leadership is accustomed to seeing these data in graph form, a chart such as the one in Figure 2.1 can easily be prepared.

FASB requirements

In June 1993, the FASB issued Statement No. 117, Financial Statements for Not-for-Profit Organizations. Essentially, "This Statement . . . requires classification of an organization's net assets and its revenues, expenses, gains, and losses based on the existence or absence of donor-imposed restrictions. It requires that the amounts for each of three classes of net assets—permanently restricted, temporarily restricted, and unrestricted—be displayed in a statement of financial position." Charitable gifts, then, must be classified as having a temporary restriction, a permanent restriction, or be unrestricted.

To simplify this FASB ruling, here are some definitions presented in lay terms (be sure to consult with finance staff and auditors to address questions about specific contributions and gift accounting procedures in your organization):

• *Temporary restriction:* A donor requires that his or her gift be used to fund a specific need, such as helping purchase a piece of equipment, renovate a facility, offset a salary, or meet another need. These gifts may also be in response to a proposal or appeal letter that requests that gifts be made for a unique program or capital need.

• *Permanent restriction:* Gifts with this restriction are more commonly referred to as endowments. A donor indicates that his or her contribution must not be spent (therefore having a permanent restriction), but that all or part of its income (and/or growth) may

Figure 2.1. Revenue per employee: ABC Hospital vs. ABC Foundation

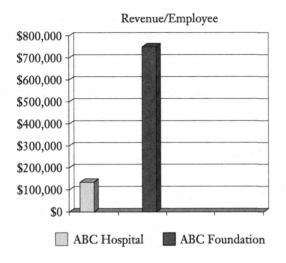

be used by the organization. When making the gift, the donor may restrict the income or growth for a particular program or leave it to the discretion of the organization as to how the income or growth is to be used.

• *Unrestricted:* A donor makes a gift without any restrictions (there are no temporary restrictions and no permanent restrictions). Making a gift payable to ABC Hospital Foundation without specifying a use or for the "programs and services of ABC Hospital Foundation" allows the foundation to use the gift for operating needs or where the foundation's board may designate. Many colleges and universities conduct annual fund campaigns that encourage unrestricted gifts to offset operating costs. This is less common in health care, as many donors respond with their largest gifts to appeals for "urgent and compelling needs" they define, thereby falling into the temporary restricted category.

Budgeting practices of each organization vary depending on its financial performance and needs. In some, the CDO may be asked to project fundraising results based on the type of restriction, if any, on the funds to be raised. This allocation of fundraising into the three FASB classifications should be based on the development office's role in meeting the organization's mission and vision, a realistic assessment of the types of appeals to be offered, what donors are most likely to respond to, board policies, and other factors.

For the $3,750,000 in funds raised by ABC Hospital Foundation (see Exhibit 2.1), the CDO may have provided the following projections as part of the hospital's budgeting process (the foundation's operating expenses are funded by a number of sources including investment income):

Temporary restricted	$3,000,000
Permanently restricted	$250,000
Unrestricted	$500,000

Integrating fundraising into the annual budget process

The strategic planning process can prioritize, align, and unite the goals of an organization's many constituencies. A similar tactic can be applied to the annual budgeting process, based on a five-step approach defined by fundraising executives Janet DeWolfe, Joseph F. Hansen, and Robert H. Greenwood (2003):

1. Meet with hospital administration annually to identify and prioritize all major capital and program needs.
2. Review what major needs might be most appealing to potential donors.
3. Evaluate, discuss, prioritize, and select needs for fundraising.
4. Meet with department directors whose projects would benefit from fundraising to review their needs and the benefits.
5. Prepare case statements for individual needs.

Oakwood Healthcare System Foundation in Dearborn, Michigan, also incorporates philanthropy into its annual budgeting process. Oakwood's leadership has formalized the selection process and uses eight criteria for assessing whether a budget request will be funded through the foundation (O'Malley and Gray, 2004):

- Mission alignment
- System strategic alignment
- Innovation
- Limited or no other source of funding
- Community/board support
- Advances clinic education and research
- Advances training of physicians, employees, and volunteers
- Philanthropically appealing

Oakwood evaluates each budget request according to its community benefit and uses these six metrics (O'Malley and Gray, 2004):

- Supports the organization's community-based mission
- Targets the problems of the poor or medically underserved
- Improves the health status of the identified community
- Reduces community health costs
- Is accessible to the entire community regardless of ability to pay
- Stimulates external community partnerships

Oakwood's leadership says the advantages of this formalized process include being better able to identify prioritized needs, define funding gaps, provide more time to match donors to needs, and increase support to those in need (O'Malley and Gray, 2004). The program's leadership is considering strengthening this model by allowing midyear requests and defining endowment goals.

Another way to contribute to the success of these two approaches (the five-step process leading to case statements for individual needs and the Oakwood model) is for the CDO to increase his or her understanding of the interests, motivations, and recognition needs of the organization's best potential donors by conducting a major gifts interest survey (Costa, 2004). Essentially, the survey is a form of field reconnaissance that gives donors the opportunity to advise fundraising leadership on how to best succeed not only in meeting the organization's financial needs, but also in designing and shaping its programs so they are tailored to the donor's charitable interests. This feedback also helps determine which budget requests are likely to attract the highest levels of support and provides parameters for designing and developing a major gifts program.

Those who are interested in creating an interest survey might ask the following questions when meeting with potential donors:

• Do you think we are an organization that could attract major gift support?
• When you think of a major gift on an annual basis, what amount comes to mind?
• When you make a major gift to another charity, what benefits do you receive? Which benefits do you value most? What specific benefits do you think we should offer?
• Are there specific services or programs that we offer that you would like to support? Or do you prefer to allow our organization to direct your gift where it is needed most?
• If we were to start a major gift program, who do you think we should recruit to lead it?

Results from a survey at one organization not only revealed several large gift opportunities but created the basis of a leadership giving group. Many of these donors said that for annual major gifts, there was no need to restrict these gifts for specific projects. "As long as I believe your organization is well run, it doesn't matter to me how you spend it," was a comment that was heard repeatedly. (For capital campaigns, there was a preference for knowing where gifts were being directed.) Among the conclusions of this interest survey were these:

• A core group who would make unrestricted gifts of ten thousand dollars per year, with a smaller group who had individual preferences where they would like to designate their giving (for instance, cancer or cardiology)

- The need for this group to be perceived as annual leadership donors
- A clear picture of the specific recognition benefits they would like to receive

Underwriting other operating and capital needs

In addition to providing mission-driven support through major gift campaigns, the annual budgeting process, and leadership giving clubs, there are at least four additional ways development can partner with finance and the organization's donors: existing temporary restricted funds, role of fundraising in borrowing funds, long-term stability through planned gifts and endowments, and supply-side philanthropy.

Existing temporary restricted funds

Most health care organizations have accumulated temporary restricted funds (sometimes referred to as special-purpose funds) over the years. The restrictions on these contributions may be as general as "capital equipment needs for the surgery department." As a good steward, the hospital must use these funds as the donors have intended. If an organization is not using these funds, one orderly way to meet this goal is for development staff to work with the finance department to identify the purpose or restrictions of each fund and then analyze the annual budget requests (operating and capital) to determine if any of the requests meet the restrictions on these funds. A spreadsheet can be prepared that identifies the restricted fund number (assigned by the finance department), the name of the fund, source of funding (the donor's name), the fund's purposes or restrictions, fund balance, amount of the proposed expenditure, and its use or purpose. Research should include a careful study of the original gift agreements or letters that created these funds. It also may be necessary to consult with finance staff, the organization's attorney, and auditors if there are significant questions about the donors' restrictions and use of specific funds. At one hospital, more than $4 million in program and capital needs during one budget year was met by this process.

Role of fundraising in borrowing funds

By maintaining the highest possible bond rating, a health care organization will lower the cost of borrowing funds and ensure a successful sale of its bonds. Documenting the history and continuity of generous community support often conveys to the lending community and investors that the organization has added stability and suggests that if there are financial problems in the future, contributors will rally to assist to protect it. Tucked in the narrative of such negative topics as medical malpractice, litigation, and payments for municipal services, one hospital's offering statement says, "During fiscal years ended June 30, 2001 and 2002, the Hospital and Foundation received more than $33.8 million in campaign contributions, life income gifts and bequests. The last major building campaign . . . raised $29.6 million, as compared to the Hospital's original goal of $17 million. The Hospital and Foundation have continuously been the beneficiaries of generous gifts, bequests, and other deferred gifts and have received strong financial support from the community in all their fundraising efforts" (Abington Memorial Hospital Obligated Group, 2002). Not surprisingly, this hospital's bonds sold quickly and with a bond rating that is favorable to the organization.

Long-term stability through planned gifts and endowments

Planned giving professional Jane Rae Bradford, director of gift planning at Carnegie Mellon University, likes to point out that for most donors, annual gifts often are made from the donor's income—perhaps a gift written from a checking account. By contrast, major and planned gifts tend to be much larger in size and are made from assets. They are like having a savings account to help make a special purchase or meet an urgent need. We can count on these assets to be there when we need them.

An organization's "savings account to help make a special purchase or meet a rainy day emergency" could very well be its planned giving program, which encourages donors to make bequests, fund life income gifts and trusts, and consider other ways to protect its good work well into the future. Unrestricted planned gifts or perhaps gifts toward endowments can benefit an organization in both good and bad times.

An easy way to start a planned giving program is with a recognition membership society or with a simple brochure that makes donors aware of why a will is needed and the personal benefits it provides. This brochure can be used in mailings or, depending on the sensitivity of donors, included with thank-you letters for gifts to an annual giving program.

Education and promotion programs also may be designed to educate trustees, doctors, and other major contributors of the benefits of establishing endowments that provide an added level of income well into the future for the organization.

Supply-side philanthropy

It is not unusual to hear of a contributor who has a special project or interest and approaches a charity to discuss whether it will help meet that need. "Donors want to be involved and to express themselves through their gifts," says Gene Tempel (2002), executive director of the Center on Philanthropy at Indiana University. Tempel explains that in demand-side philanthropy, which is sometimes labeled supply-side philanthropy, an organization enlists donors to support its goals or projects. By contrast, the supply-side model starts with the donor with ideas who is searching for institutions to implement them and achieve his or her dream. Tempel believes that the fundraiser's role is to mediate these two positions (the donor's supply with the institution's demand), thereby building a partnership between the donor and institution.

Clearly, some organizations and their finance staff welcome the opportunity to explore supply-side gift opportunities. But not all organizations are open to donors who are seeking to restrict gifts for particular programs, and not all program requests are consistent with an organization's mission.

If the request is outside the budgeting process, among the questions to be asked are:

- Is the donor's request consistent with the organization's interests, mission, and vision?
- Is this a need that has traditionally been unmet solely due to lack of funding?
- Would this enhance the organization's effectiveness or instead divert staff away from key projects and priorities?

If the organization has adopted the Oakwood model for evaluating projects, another question is:

- How well does this request meet our grant-making criteria?

The leadership of the organization and its finance staff must be willing to have an open and objective discussion of these gift opportunities if it is to engage supply-side donors.

Partnership opportunities

Despite pressures on an organization's finance and development departments, these two services can partner in ways that develop strong relationships with donors by focusing on the organization's mission and vision. Reporting tools used by finance may not meet the needs of development, and it is reasonable for it to present its goals, progress, and fundraising results in ways that increase understanding by board members and other constituents. There are also reporting tools and metrics to demonstrate that fundraising has a favorable and significantly high return for the budget dollars invested.

Fundraising can assume a central role in providing resources necessary to implement the organization's strategic plan, enhance its annual operating and capital budget, and even obtain a favorable bond placement. Through leadership giving clubs, use of current temporary restricted funds, planned gifts, and even supply-side philanthropy, donors can be engaged in ways that further the organization's vision, potential, and success.

References

Abelson, R. "Demand, But No Capital, at Nonprofit Hospitals." *New York Times*, June 21, 2002.

Abington Memorial Hospital Obligated Group. "Offering Statement for New Issue $145,000,000 Montgomery County Higher Education and Health Authority (Pennsylvania), Hospital Revenue Bonds, Series A of 2002." New York: Solomon Smith Barney, Oct. 10, 2002.

Advisory Board Company. *Special Report: Elevating Philanthropy: Exceptional Practice in Major-Donor Fundraising.* Washington, D.C.: Advisory Board Company, 2003.

Costa, N. G. *Dream Builders: Everything You Need to Know to Achieve Your Organization's Most Ambitious Dreams with TOP GIFTS Fundraising.* Danbury, Conn.: E3 Fundraising, 2004.

DeWolfe, J., Hansen, J. F., and Greenwood, R. H. "Going to the Next Level: Changing Your Institution's Focus on Philanthropy to Dramatically Increase the Size and Number of Major Gifts." Paper presented to the Thirty-Seventh Annual Association for Healthcare Philanthropy International Educational Conference, San Francisco, Oct. 2003.

Financial Accounting Standards Board. *Financial Statements for Not-for-Profit Organizations.* Norwalk, Conn.: Financial Accounting Standards Board, June 1993.

INDEPENDENT SECTOR. *A Survey of Charitable Giving After September 11, 2001.* Washington, D.C.: INDEPENDENT SECTOR, 2002.

O'Malley, C., and Gray, N. "Talking the Hospital's CFO Language." Paper presented at the Thirty-Eighth Annual Association for Healthcare Philanthropy International Educational Conference, New Orleans, Sept. 2004.

Tempel, G. "Fundraising: Obstacles and Opportunities," *Commonwealth Quarterly*, Winter 2002, pp. 4–5.

NICK G. COSTA *is a fundraising executive who regularly contributes to the profession with articles, presentations, and, recently, a book on major gifts fundraising.*

Effective stewardship is one of the best ways to reduce donor attrition, increase revenue, and decrease costs. It is a powerful element in winning and retaining donors who have the continued ability to make major gifts.

3

Successful strategies for effective stewardship

L. Alayne Metrick

IN TODAY'S NONPROFIT SECTOR, the success of many organizations and their future growth potential is defined to a large extent by the effectiveness of their fundraising. Those of us in the health care development profession have been fortunate to experience an increase in our revenues. Yet at the same time, there is a correlating increase in the cost of fundraising. We are further challenged by increased involvement from knowledgeable donors who are closely scrutinizing the balance sheets of foundations to ensure that their dollars are being invested wisely and that their gifts are providing valuable benefits within the most effective programs.

Effective stewardship is one of the best ways to reduce donor attrition, increase revenue, decrease costs, decrease cost per dollar raised, and move more donors up the pyramid. Although every donor, no matter how small or large their donation, must be appreciated and treated with the utmost respect, there are some additional

NEW DIRECTIONS FOR PHILANTHROPIC FUNDRAISING, NO. 49, FALL 2005 © WILEY PERIODICALS, INC.

stewardship implications for the top third of donors in any organization. I refer to this group as the Top Three Percent of donors.

In any discussion about the Top Third, it is appropriate to reference Jerold Panas. In his book *Megagifts* (1984), he discusses the "Rule of Thirds": one-third of the funds in any campaign will come from the top 10 to 15 gifts, another third from the next 100 to 125 gifts, and the remaining third from all other gifts. The lesson for campaign planners to learn is that while planning a campaign, it is absolutely critical to be successful at generating the top 10 to 15 gifts as well as the next 100 to 125 in order to meet the campaign goal.

This chapter demonstrates that although there is no magic formula to open doors and checkbooks, the concept of effective stewardship can be a powerful element in winning and retaining donors who have the continuing ability to make major gifts.

At St. Michael's Hospital, a research study that we undertook provided valuable lessons about the most effective use of donor-centered techniques and how to identify the right donors for applying these techniques. Somewhat unique in our industry, our hypothesis was based on improving the attrition rates of first-time donors through a donor-centered approach. This research led to some interesting observations that challenge some of the previous thinking in our industry.

Challenging the status quo

In *Thanks! A Guide to Donor-Centred Fundraising* (2000), Penelope Burk discusses issues of concern to the fundraising industry and strongly urges that fundraisers focus on "increasing the philanthropic value of donors who are already giving" (p. 6). She also notes that "50 percent of donors stop giving within a year and almost 90 percent disappear within five years" (p. 7). In a four-year study involving over one hundred donors; charities with small, medium, and large donor bases; and one hundred interviews with individual, corporate, and foundation donors, Burk found that donors want:

- Prompt acknowledgment of their gift
- Confirmation that their gifts have been used in the way that was initially communicated to them
- Sometime between gift acknowledgment and the next ask, measurable results of their gifts at work

Although Burk was applying this research to a direct mail clientele, she believes these learnings are applicable to other forms of donor solicitations such as acquisition appeals. The premise in her book is that if these donor requirements are fully met, the result will be a drop in donor attrition and an increase in retention. Her theory emphasizes that "over time those who can give more will in fact give more, and revenue will dramatically increase" (p. 11).

Inspired by this book, we decided to conduct a research study at St. Michael's Hospital Foundation. We began a study of donor-centered principles, hoping that we could find new donors to move up the giving pyramid from small to larger gifts. As a starting point, we reviewed the literature, including Burk's book, and compiled best practices from across Canada, making the decision to focus on measurement of results.

Although we did identify a number of best practices, we also found that due to a lack of time and resources, shops are only at the beginning stages of analyzing attrition rates.

Within St. Michael's Hospital Foundation, we looked at our gross revenue over the past ten years. Although we were doing well, with a steady year-over-year improvement, our attrition rate was steadily increasing as well. Given that St. Michael's Hospital is a teaching hospital affiliated with the world-renowned University of Toronto, we decided we could tap into our academic resources to develop a research study that would be of benefit to our shop and could be shared among others. We were fortunate enough to enlist the assistance of Art Slutsky, the vice president of research, and

Aiala Barr, research scientist, at St. Michael's Hospital who worked with us to develop the research design including the development of a hypothesis, approach, and methodology of our research study.

Our hypothesis, or the specific expectation we wished to test through research, was the following:

- By implementing donor-centered fundraising, we will reduce donor attrition in first-time donors from 62 percent to 55 percent.
- By involving board members in the process of thanking donors, their personal giving will increase.
- Over a period of time, this approach will have a positive impact on our major gifts program.

We hoped that this overall initiative would have a positive impact on our major gift process, enabling us to find donors who would move up the giving pyramid.

To test our hypothesis, the initial research design was launched in two phases, in the spring and fall of 2002. Working with the planning department at St. Michael's Hospital, we launched the research project to coincide with an acquisition appeal to raise funds for the construction of a new fracture clinic within the hospital. As part of the research design, we divided donors into two groups as their donations arrived: a control group and a test group. Based on our goal to recruit one thousand first-time donors into this study, we grouped 492 donors into the control group and 537 into the test group. We assigned donors to their respective group prior to opening the correspondence from them.

In order to test the thank-you model, all donors in both the control and the test groups received a thank-you letter and a receipt within twenty-four to forty-eight hours of receiving their donation. Each donor also received a newsletter and our most recent direct mail piece. This is where the similarities ended.

The test group received key elements as recommended in Burk's donor-centered fundraising approach: a thank-you call from either a staff or a board member, ideally within twenty-four to forty-eight hours, and a follow-up accountability component by letter, a document we referred to as a status report. This information piece was personalized with an actual signature, addressed the donor throughout the letter, included a patient testimonial, and was mailed out eight weeks after the receipt of the gift. Positive and upbeat in tone, it reported on measurable impacts and provided meaningful information about what the renovations would mean to patients.

As we implemented the research, we were able to determine the demographics of the control and test group, and this led to an understanding of our typical donor profile. This is extremely useful information when targeting specific marketing and communication strategies to meet the needs of the audience. Given the similarities of the two groups, we were assured that the results of the thank-you initiative would be unbiased based on the demographic factors of gender, age, and average household income.

Research results

The results were not necessarily what we were expecting; however, they were interesting, and we can take some learnings away from them.

By linking each finding back to our original hypothesis, we can easily determine what we learned. Our first hypothesis was, "By implementing donor-centered fundraising, we will reduce donor attrition in first-time donors from 62 percent to 55 percent." The renewal rate of donors in both the control and the test groups was largely the same (29 percent and 24 percent, respectively). By this, we can conclude that the attrition rate was virtually the same despite the additional intervention of a personal telephone call from either a board or staff member.

We also wanted to determine whether the personal phone call and the accountability status report had any impact on the size of the renewal gifts given by our donors. We found that the percentage of donors who chose to keep their same level of support or decrease their level of support with the second gift remained virtually the same in both the control and the test groups. However, there was a slight increase in the percentage of donors in the test group who decided to increase their level of support with a renewal gift: from 17 percent in the control group to 23 percent in the test group. This was a positive finding and might lead us to believe that the call to say thank-you does make an impact on the decision to increase the level of support.

As we analyzed the research findings, we also wanted to determine if the size of the gift was affected by whether the thank-you call was placed by a board member or a staff member. The results indicate that this made absolutely no difference at all in the size of the gift.

Our next hypothesis was that "by involving board members, their personal giving will increase." Our board members indicated that overall, the people they spoke to were appreciative of the call and were surprised by it. They believed it was an excellent idea and a powerful tool that can be taken into the future. All board members who participated have continued to give to our foundation through pledge payments or cash gifts to special events or have made additional pledges to our current research-capital campaign. Finally, we sought to determine if this approach would have a positive impact on our major gifts program over a period of time. For the purposes of this study, we determined that a major gift would be defined as a gift of $10,000 or more. As of February 2005, the control group had one donor who made a major gift, and the test group had three individuals who made a gift of ten thousand dollars or more. We attribute this increase to the personal phone call. In addition, both the control group and the test group generated two planned gifts. Another interesting insight was that the value of the planned gifts generated through the test group was significantly higher than those in the control group, leading us to believe that our interventions did contribute to a higher level of planned giving.

Lessons learned from our research

Here is what we learned from the research project:

- Timely telephone calls are critical to success. Donors are not particularly receptive to a call that is not prompt and may feel that it is another solicitation.
- The time period between solicitations needed to be shortened. Our next appeal was mailed from nine to twelve months following the call. Given the time lapse, many donors did not remember the thank-you call or the status report.
- Time management is key to the process. Since time essentially translates into dollars, we learned that the more personalized and time-sensitive donor-centered techniques should be reserved for major gifts.

Prior to testing, we had assumed that all donors, regardless of the size of their donation, would benefit from an understanding of how money is spent and from a personal call. From our results, we can infer that in fact donors who are giving smaller gifts are annoyed with the amount of attention they receive for a gift that they assumed was not a major one.

Our key learning from this research is that donor-centered techniques should be reserved for major gifts.

Winning strategies for securing the Top Three Percent

It is important to fully understand the personality traits and interests of the Top Three Percent. The individuals in this group are used to getting what they want and are high achievers both personally and professionally. They are incredibly focused, results oriented, and inspired by winning organizations that can demonstrate meaningful results—and quickly.

The Top Three Percent are interested in leaving a personal and a lasting legacy on the organizations they support. *The Seven Faces of Philanthropy* (1994) by Russ Alan Prince and Karen Maru File has an interesting perspective on donor personalities. It is a notion that reinforces the importance of analyzing the donor audience characteristics and developing specifically targeted strategies responsive to their unique needs. Prince and File identified these philanthropic personalities:

- The Communitarian—doing good makes sense
- The Devout—doing good is God's will
- The Investor—doing good is good business
- The Socialite—doing good is fun
- The Altruist—doing good feels right
- The Repayer—doing good in return
- The Dynasty—doing good is a family tradition

Determining the predominant personality profile of the individuals in their own Top Three Percent will help fundraisers to understand their motivation for giving and provide a framework for developing targeted marketing and communication strategies and recognition events that meet their needs.

Here are some of the best practices we have leveraged with success for recruiting and maintaining the Top Three Percent:

- Keep them involved and engaged. For example, invite them to celebrations and special events even if you know they will not attend.
- Help them develop relationships with more than one representative of the institution. This means you are pivotal, but introduce them to the CEO, interesting and knowledgeable staff experts, and key volunteer leadership.
- Have something relevant to talk to them about. This might require some research and advance work, but when you have them captive, you need to talk about something other than the weather or the baseball scores to ensure they remain engaged and interested.

- Give the most exciting opportunities to major donors. They will appreciate the chance to have the first option at funding something unique.
- Ensure they understand the organization's mission and vision. You can help them do this through telephone calls, personal visits, and letters.
- Share your successes. Winners love being associated with other winners. You can keep them up-to-date through newsletters, circulating news clippings that profile your success, and annual reports, for example.
- Identify other friends or associates who may know the individual well. They can be an excellent resource in terms of the person's likes and dislikes and what type of project has the greatest likelihood of getting funded.
- Use a gift agreement to help ensure everyone is in agreement and to alleviate any later misunderstandings.
- Say thank-you many times, and involve many people in the process.

The role of the major gift officer, and that of the board members, is also critical to a successful Top Three Percent strategy. As the subject expert, the major gift officer needs to articulate the cause, explain the crucial facts and figures, and make the dream and the vision appear to be a potential reality for the donor. This is especially critical because hospital foundations are in continual campaign mode as donors often decide to show their support through a pledge, and the next campaign may in fact be launched before they finish their current one. The major gifts officer also has a pivotal role in ensuring that meaningful recognition strategies are coordinated and implemented.

Keep in mind that most donors want recognition, and it is important to determine from donors the kind of recognition that is not only appropriate for the organization but also meaningful to them. Often a celebration or grand opening for those who are funding a major project can be twinned with a recognition event.

This gives the donor the opportunity to receive public thanks from the president and CEO and other senior leadership, and from board members. They will also have the opportunity to interact with individuals such as patients and their families, who can be extremely effective in sharing their stories and experiences of how the gift will directly benefit their lives.

Role of key stakeholders, including board members and physicians

Board members and physicians are two key stakeholder groups that are extremely influential and provide major contributions to the fundraising success we have experienced at St. Michael's Hospital. Their support is pivotal. We have involved both the board and our physicians in our major fundraising strategies, and we believe it has paid off twofold: in increasing the value of the gifts that are brought into the foundation and in enriching the satisfaction and owner-ship of these two groups.

Our board leadership becomes involved in a number of ways. Often they have a relationship with a potential donor and are able to open the door, providing an entry point and an introduction for staff to create the vision and therefore make the request. We encourage them to accompany staff on key calls whenever possible. The support and endorsement of board members cannot be under-estimated. As volunteers who are passionate about the cause they represent, they provide third-party credibility and authenticity for the organization. We ensure that board members are also included in the recognition event and that they have the opportunity to say thank-you as well.

At St. Michael's Hospital, we are fortunate to have a staff of physicians who provide excellent and compassionate patient care and are also involved in research and teaching activities. Many of our donors give their initial gift as a mark of appreciation to their physician, but continue to give because of their continued relationship with the institution. This is where foundation staff can build on the rapport that many patients enjoy with their doctor and use stewardship and recognition activities to bring them along to the next level of giving.

Profiling the success of physicians becomes an extremely important tool in communicating with donors. When research is published in medical journals or a physician is featured or quoted in a mainstream newspaper article or publication, copies are sent to the donor in a timely fashion to help reinforce the cause, and the continued outcomes, of their support.

Leveraging public relations for success

It is crucial to develop a close relationship and partnership with your organization's public relations or communications department. Many of the strategic tools executed by the public relations function—annual reports, newsletters and other publications, and the Web site, to name just a few—will be pivotal to demonstrating not only the organization's mission and future directions but the value of donors' gifts, and therefore they can be effectively leveraged to communicate your key messages.

Working together will ensure that messages are consistent and reinforced and will add credibility and authenticity to your efforts. At St. Michael's Hospital, for example, we hold regular meetings to highlight upcoming events and brainstorm around ideas that can recognize donors and profile their good works externally. We are involved in the planning of major initiatives such as the Web site, annual report, and other publications to ensure that our needs are represented as part of the overall big picture. We work extremely closely with the person responsible for the media relations function to identify newsworthy stories, articles, events, or opportunities that will not only profile the organization but interest potential donors or recognize an existing donor in a unique and public way.

Lessons learned

In summary, here is what we have learned and have applied to our fundraising strategies with respect to the Top Three Percent of donors:

• Donor-centered fundraising techniques are most successful and cost-effective when they are used to develop relationships with the Top Three Percent of your donors.

• Understanding of your organization can be significantly enhanced for donors if you help them develop relationships with key individuals such as the president and CEO, other board members, physicians, and other major donors. These new linkages will complement the existing relationship with the major gift officer, who is ultimately responsible for ensuring effective stewardship at all of these levels.

• Stewardship is critical to fundraising success. Effective relationship building includes recognition whenever appropriate, continued thanks and appreciation, and ongoing cultivation.

• Understand the motives, values, and personal preferences of major gift donors so that you can continue to inspire their spirit of philanthropy. Through a better understanding of their interests, you can develop and recommend gift opportunities that are relevant to them and also support the organization's strategic priorities.

• A well-integrated marketing and communications plan can help to reinforce key messages, themes, and needs for your organization and can provide donors with the personal satisfaction that comes from acknowledging they have made a wise investment with lasting benefits.

• The benefit of research cannot be underestimated. Research, when conducted in a thoughtful and methodical way, is a meaningful addition to the body of knowledge in fundraising. In challenging times, it becomes an important tool to help fundraisers make the best use of resources.

There may not be a magic bullet to open the doors and check-books of your Top Three Percent, but there is a time-honored solution that will open hearts—the best place to start. Effective stewardship is essentially the application of simple human values that have endured over time: dignity, respect, and creating a feeling of community and of trust for donors. Combined with the strategies outlined in this chapter, these relationship-building values will give you the influence you need to raise your organization's fundraising potential to a powerful new level.

References

Burk, P. *Thanks! A Guide to Donor-Centred Fundraising.* Burlington, Ontario: Burk and Associates, 2000.

Metrick, A., and Mourinho, M. "Impacting Donor Attrition Rates." Toronto: St. Michael's Hospital Foundation Research Study, 2002.

Panas, J. *Megagifts: Who Gives Them, Who Gets Them.* Santa Monica, Calif.: Bonus Books, 1984.

Prince, A. R., and File, K. M. *The Seven Faces of Philanthropy: A New Approach to Cultivating Major Donors.* San Francisco: Jossey-Bass, 1994.

L. ALAYNE METRICK *is president of St. Michael's Hospital Foundation in Toronto, Ontario, Canada.*

Truly savvy CEOs have grasped the importance of devoting resources to philanthropy.

4

The fundraising CEO

Frank R. Hall

BEFORE THE ADVENT OF Medicare and Medicaid, hospital fundraising in the United States was pretty much confined to building new structures. A hospital administrator was responsible for keeping physicians happy and for carrying out the mission of whichever group, often religious, sponsored the hospital.

Immediately after World War II, two things happened that accelerated the need for fundraising campaigns in American community hospitals. First, the young people who had fought in the war came home and began the baby boom. Hospital beds were in critically short supply everywhere, so Congress passed the Hill-Burton Act to provide funds to assist hospitals in building structures to house more beds. Hill-Burton grants were matching grants: in order to get the money, the community had to conduct a campaign to raise funds in order to get the government grant.

Second, the era of medical technology began, and expensive new equipment became available. For the first time, some hospitals borrowed money to buy equipment because the cost was so high. Some community hospitals in the early 1960s began to hire full-time fundraising staff and create separate fundraising arms, often called foundations, to conduct fundraising on a continuous basis. Still, almost all fundraising was conducted by volunteers, some with

NEW DIRECTIONS FOR PHILANTHROPIC FUNDRAISING, NO. 49, FALL 2005 © WILEY PERIODICALS, INC.

and some without the advice and organizational assistance of a fundraising professional.

As hospitals became more sophisticated, administrators became more professional and had greater responsibility. Their title became "executive director."

Universities began to add graduate schools of health care administration. The passage of Medicare made health care a business, and investor-owned hospital chains became the darlings of Wall Street. Increasingly, hospitals borrowed.

Hospital foundations and fundraising departments referred to their efforts as "providing a margin of excellence." This implied that the bottom line of the hospital was adequate to provide most capital needs, so philanthropic support would be used to provide the extras.

As health care management became more complex, the executive director became president and CEO. Often a chief operating officer was hired to run the operation while the president and CEO increasingly dealt with physician and community relationships.

Still, a student could get a doctorate in health care administration and never have a single lecture on fundraising.

In Canada, meanwhile, the advent of the National Health Plan made fundraising unnecessary until the late 1970s, when provincial politicians discovered that hospitals could depend on gifts from their communities to make up capital budget shortfalls. The more the government cut the capital budget, the more the community raised.

Soon after, and seemingly overnight, things began to change for American hospitals. The federal government threw up its hands in exasperation over trying to control hospital costs and switched to payment by diagnosis-related group. From then on, the hospital made money on Medicare patients only if it could gain control of costs. Simultaneously, insurance companies were given the right to negotiate rates with hospitals. The term *managed care* was coined to describe the new situation in which a third party (most often a health maintenance organization representative) participated in the decision about the care of a doctor's patient. In response, hospitals formed themselves into "health systems" to gain more bargaining power.

There are only three sources of capital for nonprofit hospitals: the bottom line, borrowing, and philanthropy. A significant percentage of hospitals found themselves unable to make a profit on operations sufficient to cover the increased need for capital. Borrowing became more expensive as the lack of profits forced down bond ratings. Almost overnight, hospital philanthropy became a lifeline to survival.

In the thirty-five years between the advent of Medicare and the turn of the twenty-first century, American hospitals went from cash cow to cash poor. All of a sudden, hospital presidents and CEOs became vitally interested in increasing philanthropic support for their institutions, which in many cases had little history of community support.

Truly savvy CEOs soon grasped the importance of devoting resources to the development of a philanthropic base on which to build for the future. They realized that they would have to spend money to raise money, and if they wanted philanthropy to begin to play a major role in providing capital for their institution, they were going to have to begin to pay a lot more attention to it. Unfortunately, most CEOs were too busy trying to keep their institutions in the black. Only recently have they begun to grasp the need for their personal commitment to philanthropic development, and they are scrambling to catch up.

Donors have changed too. Once content to check off a box on the envelope titled "where needed most," donors are now very specific about how they want their money spent, and major donors want to meet and converse with the people who will be spending their money. They do not want to talk to a department manager or professional fundraiser; they want to discuss their gift with the CEO.

The role of the physician today

Years ago, every hospital campaign started with a campaign to gain significant gifts from physicians. They were the people who most understood the need for support and were often among the most affluent in the community. That is no longer the case.

Today physicians are facing higher costs for their practice and lower reimbursement and often find themselves estranged from and even competing with their hospitals. Yet it is physicians who develop relationships with their patients and are in the best position to influence grateful patients to support the hospital. In most hospitals, the person best able to cultivate physician participation in the philanthropic process is the CEO.

Developing a philanthropic culture

To raise the massive amounts needed in the United States and Canada, nonprofit hospitals will have to develop a philanthropic culture. Consultant Karla Williams (1999) has written, "Notable differences exist between organizations that achieve success in fundraising and those that do not. But, the primary and most obvious difference is the presence of, or lack of, a Philanthropic Culture" (p. 16). Culture change is possible only with the 100 percent dedicated support of the hospital's senior management led by the CEO.

As health care institutions have evolved, so have hospital foundations and resource development offices. In the early days of hospital fundraising, chief development officers were often also in charge of the hospital's public relations department. It was a rare hospital that had more than four or five people employed full time in fundraising. Today, larger foundations in the United States and Canada have twenty or more.

Early foundation fundraising activities had a heavy emphasis on special events and support organizations such as guilds and auxiliaries. Today's hospital fundraising professionals are better educated, they are members of and most often certified by the Association for Healthcare Philanthropy, and they have a much longer tenure in fundraising than their predecessors. They are likely to be specialists holding titles such as "major gifts officer," "capital campaign director," "director of planned giving," or "annual giving coordinator." The fundraising staff is likely to be much larger, because a lot more money must be raised.

Still, this enlarged fundraising staff is not going to achieve ambitious goals without the participation of just about everyone in the hospital. Doctors, nurses, technicians, volunteers, admitting clerks, and bill collectors (to name just a few) play a significant role in determining the attitude the patient or prospect takes away from his or her experience with the hospital. There is a role to play for everyone associated with the institution. How and if they accept that role will depend in great measure on the influence of the chief executive officer.

CEOs are accepting this responsibility, but they want to know how they can be effective. To outline the role of the CEO in the fundraising function, we developed a fund development job description for chief executive officers in our health system. Part of the description is as follows:

A Chief Executive Officer's Fund Development Job Description

Culture of Philanthropy

The Chief Executive must be the Chief Architect in the creation of a "culture of philanthropy" in the institution. This means that every single individual associated with the hospital—whether manager, employee, physician or volunteer—participates in the Fund Development process by being aware that the hospital is a charitable enterprise worthy of philanthropic support. This can be accomplished by seeing that:

1. Employees who have public contact are trained to refer grateful patients and their families to the Foundation for follow-up.
2. Fund Development maintains a prominent place on the agenda for management, physician and staff meetings as well as Trustee meetings and retreats.
3. Every publication produced contains references to the importance of philanthropy to the institution.
4. All management staff members have personal goals which encourage them to promote the institution's success in fundraising.
5. Employee and Board Orientation programs include a philanthropic component.
6. All successful fund development activities are praised and celebrated and persons responsible for that success are recognized.
7. All Executive Management Team members participate eagerly and actively in fund development activities as appropriate. This includes

attendance at both fundraising and cultivation events; vendor solicitation; speaking to public community and business groups as part of a hospital speakers bureau; and acting as hosts or tour guides for visiting donors and prospects.

8. Provide an update of Philanthropic support to the employees on a regular basis, no less often than annually.

Physician Participation

The majority of major gifts to hospitals are made by grateful patients and their family members. As far as those prospective donors are concerned, their physician is responsible for the excellent treatment they received. Physicians often play a pivotal role in philanthropic decisions by their patients. In his or her interactions with physicians the CEO should:

1. Communicate to the medical staff individually and as a group the critical role of philanthropy in providing for the future needs of the institution.
2. Encourage physicians to actively participate in the fund development program as donors, solicitors, relationship developers and spokespersons.
3. Publicly praise, recognize and celebrate physicians who do participate in the fund development program.
4. Recruit physicians to work in various capacities in the fund development program.

Community Relationship Development

As the major spokesperson for the institution, the CEO should:

1. With the input of the Public Relations and Marketing staff, work with the Fund Development Executive to develop a public presentation about the hospital and actively market this program to community groups such as service clubs. Appearances on local television and radio should also be actively sought. In each public appearance the fact that the hospital is non-profit and dependent on community support should be stressed.
2. Be prepared to meet with groups invited to tour the hospital.
3. Attend public functions (excluding fundraising events for unrelated charities) as appropriate as a representative of the hospital.
4. Act like the representative of a charitable enterprise. A successful fundraising organization cannot at the same time be a major donor to other organizations. To the extent that support of outside organizations is desirable, have the hospital appear as a "collaborator" and not a "donor."

Major Gift Development

Successful major gift fundraising doesn't occur until a potential donor has developed a relationship with the institutional leadership. Major donors have every right to expect to develop a relationship with the hospital CEO. The Hospital CEO should:

1. Make him or her available to meet with major donor prospects as requested by the Foundation Executive.
2. Participate as a member of the "Prospect Management Team" of the Foundation and accept responsibility for the ongoing cultivation of donor relationships as appropriate. A CEO may have 10, 20 or more prospects to personally "manage" through cultivation, solicitation, recognition and stewardship. This involves personal contact with the prospect/donor at each step of the relationship.
3. Make his or her home available for occasional functions as appropriate, and/or host events at outside locations.
4. Be prepared to participate as part of a solicitation team with Fund Development Staff, Physicians or Volunteer Leaders.

Fund Development Must Be a Priority

If we are to achieve the ambitious goals we have set for ourselves, creating the "Culture of Philanthropy" and "Major Gift" cultivation and solicitation must be institutional priorities. Therefore, the CEO should:

1. Put the donor first. If there is a conflict between a physician committee meeting and a major donor meeting, send the COO to the physician meeting.
2. Recognize that you are going to get back $2 or more for every $1 invested in the Foundation budget. So don't apply "across the board budget cuts" to the foundation arbitrarily. There may be times you will increase the Foundation's budget when everyone else is being cut.
3. Never forget to let donors and fundraising volunteers know how important they are to you personally and to the hospital.

What the Fund Development Staff Owes the CEO

We are asking a lot of our CEOs and here is what the Development Staff must guarantee in return:

1. The CEO's "Philanthropy" time must be carefully budgeted so that his or her time is never wasted.
2. The CEO should not be asked to "manage a relationship" with a donor who is not a "Major Donor Prospect" or with one who could

be as effectively managed by another executive at a lower level in the organization.

3. The CEO should have a right to expect good quality written information and well organized materials to work with.

4. The CEO has a right to expect that the Fund Development staff will be good stewards of hospital resources and that they will not spend money needlessly or frivolously.

Chief Executives who enthusiastically embrace the duties and responsibilities described in a CEO's fund development job description are sure to maximize their institution's philanthropic results.

Reference

Williams, K. "Climate Change." *Contributions,* July–Aug. 1999, p. 16.

FRANK R. HALL *is vice president, resource development, at St. Joseph Health System in Orange, California.*

Health care organizations must create a culture of philanthropy that includes physicians.

5

Physician fundraising: Evolution, not revolution

Mara Hook, Jerry Mapp

Physicians are trained to know the limits of their ability and to confine their activities within these limits.
—Martin Brotman, President and CEO, California Pacific Medical Center

THE IDEA OF PARTNERING physicians and philanthropy, particularly for the physicians, seems like a contradiction in terms. But any non-profit medical center serious about charting a prosperous course must create an institutional culture of philanthropy that begins with its physicians—one in which those physicians can understand and articulate the importance of philanthropy to the organization.

The best way to begin is to anoint a well-known, trusted, and respected member, or members, of the medical staff as the philanthropic pontiff for your institution. In the best of all worlds, this individual would be the CEO; however, many institutions do not have a physician CEO—and even if they are lucky enough to, that individual does not necessarily possess the skills or interest for such an assignment. The physician philanthropic pontiff could be the chair of a department or a member of the foundation or medical center board, or simply have a proven interest and some success in the fundraising arena. Once you identify this special physician, or

NEW DIRECTIONS FOR PHILANTHROPIC FUNDRAISING, NO. 49, FALL 2005 © WILEY PERIODICALS, INC.

group of physicians, who understands philanthropy, who were raised with the value of community service, or who are philanthropic themselves, you must go about the task of persuading them that they are role models for their colleagues and need to make visible the fact that they consider fundraising a necessity.

Physicians are reluctant to become fundraisers for two reasons. First, they have never done it before, and therefore they are convinced that they cannot do it. Second, and probably the greater fear, is that they have the impression that fundraising will interfere with the doctor-patient relationship.

Physician fundraising education

Physicians, like most other people, are more willing to learn something new if they can directly link their newly found knowledge to personal benefit. Make sure that your physicians understand that philanthropy in a nonprofit institution is an additional channel of funding for them outside the traditional capital and program budget process. If they are willing to work with the development professionals at their institution to participate in fundraising activities, they can directly benefit as they obtain funding for projects that are a priority for their department and the institution.

There are three forms of physician fundraising education that tend to be the most successful.

Physician-as-a-fundraiser video

A training video can be an effective way to introduce physicians to the concept of fundraising. This is also a particularly useful tool for development professionals as they attempt to engage a physician in the process. A physician fundraising video is best produced when the narrator is a respected physician at your institution. The video should offer a basic outline of the fundraising efforts at the institution, the history of fundraising success, and a specific role-play scenario between a physician and a grateful patient prospect. One of the most important roles a physician fundraiser can play is opening the door for the development staff to meet with the prospect to discuss his or her interest in a particular funding priority. The conversation in the role-play may go something like this:

PHYSICIAN: (either on the phone or in person) Helen, I am delighted with your progress. You're doing exceedingly well, and I'm thrilled to see that you are back to good health.

PATIENT: Frank and I are very grateful to you for your help, and the care at the hospital was excellent. Everyone has been most helpful.

PHYSICIAN: You know, Helen, we're always looking for better ways to take care of our patients here at the medical center. We are going to create a full-fledged cancer care center, which will include a new radiation therapy unit. I thought that possibly you and Frank would be interested in participating. You know, I don't think there is a better medical facility anywhere than this one, and a new radiation therapy unit will help so many of our patients. Would you consider meeting with me and a representative from the medical center's development staff to discuss this very important funding opportunity?

PATIENT: I think that may interest us; let me talk to Frank.

PHYSICIAN: (one week later on the phone) Helen, I promised to get back in follow-up to our conversation last week regarding your interest in supporting the medical center philanthropically.

PATIENT: Oh yes, I spoke to Frank, and he and I would love to meet to discuss the funding needs, in particular, the need for a new radiation therapy unit.

PHYSICIAN: Very good. Shall we meet in the office of development on Thursday at noon? We'll have lunch and more fully address your interest.

Typically, a development officer will have success in using the video either as a one-on-one training for physicians or to educate a group of physicians who may have a funding need in their department and understand that they will have to identify and engage their grateful patients in order to raise the required funds.

Written educational materials

If you find your physicians are not interested in watching a video or you cannot get an appointment with them to do so, it is advisable that the development staff create a clearly written collateral piece that they can offer physicians to review at their leisure or as they are working toward a solicitation meeting with a grateful patient prospect. Consider using something similar to the following list:

Top tips for physician fundraisers

- Rely on the professionals. If you have a grateful patient prospect with the potential to give, the foundation staff should always be integrally involved in planning the best course of action.
- Do your homework. Understand the project's case for support. You can work with a development professional at your institution to make sure that the case is in writing and presentable to a grateful patient prospect.
- Avoid duplicative efforts. Always inform the development staff before, during, and after approaching a prospect or undertaking any fundraising activity so that the prospect is not confused by duplicative approaches.
- Remember that grateful patients want to give. They want to say thank-you to their physician and medical center for the care they received.
- Look beyond your patient to your other contacts in the community.
- Make your own pledge first. Before you can convince others to support the medical center, you must make your own commitment as a tangible demonstration of the importance of the funding priority to you.
- See your best prospect first. The first time you make a solicitation approach, choose a grateful patient prospect whom you know well and feel comfortable approaching.
- Respond to your patient's health concerns first. Once you feel that all health concerns have been addressed, only then should you suggest a future meeting be scheduled to discuss the funding priorities of the medical center.

- Arrange the meeting in a place that is convenient for the prospect.
- Always ask for a gift in person and with a partner. It is important to invite a development professional to attend the face-to-face solicitation meeting with you. You may also want to include a volunteer board member who can serve as a peer to the prospect.
- Use your first visit to spark the prospect's interest. Approach the subject of a gift gradually. Establish common ground, and then get to the point. Be friendly, but remember this is not a social call.
- Be informative, and present the case for support. Your expertise can inspire a donor's generosity in a way that nothing else can.
- Be prepared with prospect research. You should never approach any prospect until you have an idea of this person's giving capacity and philanthropic interest. Your development staff member can provide you with this type of research.
- Always ask for a specific amount. Never say, "We have you down for this or that." Instead, say: "I'd like you to consider a gift of . . .". Make sure that, based on your prospect research, you have found out how much the prospect can give and ask for the maximum amount. It is much easier to have a prospect decrease the ask amount than to have you increase it midstream.
- Listen to your prospect. Do not get thrown off track by criticisms that the prospect might bring forth during the course of your solicitation. Many times prospects feel comfortable enough to make you aware of how they think the medical center can be improved. Offer to pass along any suggestions or criticisms, but do not get off task by responding too deeply to criticism.
- Set a definite time to discuss the gift further—in a week or ten days perhaps. People need time to make a gift decision. Plan on at least two conversations with each prospect before a gift is committed.
- Even if the response is disappointing, express your thanks. Your friendly attitude now will plant the seed for a gift in the future. "No" does not necessarily mean "no forever"; the prospect may need more information or time or may want to consider another funding priority before making a gift.

- Be proud and honored to ask. A grateful patient prospect is most likely proud and honored that you asked, so you should feel the same way. You are offering your prospect an opportunity to take part in something worthwhile and exciting.
- Always say thank-you. A prompt handwritten note or personal telephone call from you will mean more than any formal recognition that the medical center can offer.
- Relax! Your enthusiasm and sincerity are much more important than the perfection of your solicitation technique.

Direct physician involvement

One of the most important and effective ways to engage physicians in the fundraising activities of the institution is to create opportunities for them to become involved in the process. There are several ways to accomplish this objective.

First, you need to establish two core committees that encourage physician-driven funding priorities. The first is a medical center–based budget committee with a membership consisting of primarily physician leaders. This committee holds the responsibility for receiving and vetting all funding requests for the institution and considering all available sources of funding to meet those needs. By having physician members on such a committee, their sense of oversight and participation heightens; at the same time, they become educated around the sources of funding that nourish their institution.

Typically a budget committee of this type will find that it is unable to allocate enough funding to meet the needs of the entire institution. At this point, the committee members must look for additional funding sources. Physicians want the best equipment, facilities, and technology for their patients. Philanthropy enables a department to secure funding that goes above and beyond their budget. It is the icing on the cake, and as they say, that is what makes the cake taste so good! Subsequently, philanthropy becomes a top-of-mind funding stream for an institution with slim margins that wants to provide gold standard care.

As the budget committee recognizes philanthropy in this manner, it will begin to suggest funding priorities to the fundraising arm of the institution. Therefore, a second committee should be established to receive these requests, which is overseen by the foundation board or development committee.

The development committee, whose members are donors and hold volunteer leadership positions at the institution, is charged with reviewing the suggested funding priorities that have come from the physicians' budget committee. The development committee determines the fundability of the items, accepting some and rejecting others based on their knowledge of the interests of their philanthropic community. Once the most appropriate priorities have been selected, the foundation board or the development committee votes and agrees on a final list. Thus, funding priorities are created with the essential component of physician involvement and volunteer approval.

Once the funding priorities of the institution are set, yet another opportunity arises to involve physicians in the funding process. Critical to raising funds toward the funding priorities that have been set is the hands-on involvement of physician fundraisers. One way to accomplish this is by establishing a physician champion process.

The institution's funding priorities will be best approached if you consider a team approach to raising funds and completing the need. The team should have three lead champions: a volunteer leader, typically a member of the fundraising board; a respected physician who has a specific interest in the particular priority and will benefit from its funding; and a development staff member who is charged with guiding the process.

For the purposes of this chapter, we focus on the role of the physician champion. The physician champion is typically the chair of the department that requires funding, or a physician who is considered a leader by the institution and understands the need for the funding priority at hand. The physician champion is responsible for (1) making a gift toward the priority commensurate with his or her capacity; (2) soliciting, with the help of staff and the volunteer leader, all members of his or her department who will benefit from the priority; (3) bringing grateful patients to the attention of the foundation or development department who may have the capacity and interest to support the priority (the volunteer leader also brings forth names of their high-capacity friends who might have interest in making a gift); and (4) participating with the volunteer to solicit grateful patients and other prospects.

The role of the physician champion is critical to the success of the fundraising process and a culture of physician philanthropy. Physician participation sets an example for the entire medical staff and the donor community as to the importance of philanthropy to the institution. By serving as a champion, the physician tacitly informs his or her peers that physician participation leads to the funding of priorities, making available the best facilities, patient programs, medical research, and capital equipment.

Protecting the physician-patient relationship

It's 4:00 P.M. on a Friday afternoon. Dr. Smith has just finished a personal solicitation of one of his long-time patients. The meeting time had been prearranged about three weeks previous. The patient prospect was fully aware of the purpose of the meeting and willingly agreed that he and his wife would attend. The physician asks the patient prospect for a gift of $100,000 to support the cardiac catheterization lab. A week later, the physician calls the patient prospect to follow up on the solicitation, and the patient reveals that he and his wife are not in a position to make a gift. The following morning, the patient wakes up with chest pain.

Will the patient feel comfortable calling the physician? If the patient hesitates for a moment because he turned the doctor down, the doctor-patient relationship is instantly compromised. Clearly, the timing must be right for a physician to solicit a patient. The physician must feel confident that the health of the patient is stable and that no lingering health issues exist before the solicitation is made. Moreover, the physician should be provided with accurate prospect research from the development office that reflects the prospect's true ability and willingness to give.

Some physicians may have concerns about violating Health Insurance Portability and Accountability Act regulations or American Medical Association recommendations if they participate as a physician fundraiser. Or they may view such regulations as the perfect vehicle to "get them off the fundraising hook." It is important to recognize that the medical staff and the fundraising staff share a similar professional oath to protect the privacy and integrity of the community at large. Just as physicians are concerned with violating the physician-patient relationship as it pertains to health-related privacy, professional development staff are aware of protecting not only the health privacy but also the financial privacy of the donor. In fact, should a professional fundraiser not adhere to these basic tenets, the important component of donor trust is abolished, and fundraising becomes virtually impossible. To make this point to physicians, it can be quite helpful to share with the medical staff a copy of the Association for Healthcare Philanthropy Statement of Professional Standards and Conduct by which professional fundraisers are bound.

The critical difference

You cannot expect that all physicians will give or ask for gifts, but the critical difference between an institution that is "good enough" and one that is "always the best" can be philanthropy. As a professional fundraiser working with physicians, you may not be able to convince all of your medical staff to participate in raising philanthropic funds, but you should be able to expect that no physicians in your institution will ever deny the importance of philanthropy to their nonprofit medical center. With this premise as your starting point, you can make great inroads into your quest for a culture of physician fundraisers.

MARA HOOK *is vice president of development at California Pacific Medical Center Foundation in San Francisco, California.*

JERRY MAPP *is president and chief executive officer for California Pacific Medical Center Foundation in San Francisco, California.*

Accountability in fundraising often is focused on cost-benefit ratios, not how each of the individual solicitation methods performed. "How much did you raise" has been replaced with "How much did it cost?" and "How do our results compare with others'?"

6

Hardwiring for maximum fundraising return on investment

James M. Greenfield

THE ISSUE OF FUNDRAISING COST analysis has plagued nonprofit organizations, government regulators, donors, and volunteers for decades. The problem lies in two areas, each equally difficult to solve. First, the accounting profession has provided guidelines on how to conduct fundraising cost accounting by applying the "primary purpose" guideline (purpose, audience, and content) (American Institute of Certified Public Accountants, 1998, 2004). However, nonprofit auditors and fiscal officers often follow separate interpretations of these guidelines when calculating expenses reported in "Part II: Statement of Functional Expenses" in the Annual Information Return (IRS Form 990). Internal Revenue Service (IRS) instructions state clearly, "Fundraising expenses are the total expenses incurred in soliciting contributions, gifts, grants, etc." (U.S. Department of Treasury, 2004). Methods used to segregate and report these expenses are often inconsistent between auditors and

NEW DIRECTIONS FOR PHILANTHROPIC FUNDRAISING, NO. 49, FALL 2005 © WILEY PERIODICALS, INC.

fiscal officers, with the result that calculating fundraising costs has become an example of creative accounting in the extreme.

The second problem is that nonprofit organizations feel pressure to appear as efficient financial managers as well as effective in their delivery of quality programs and services. Annual reports and audited financial statements attempt to present a best-case scenario by reporting low management and fundraising costs and delude the public on whether they are good stewards of the public's money. "Savvy nonprofits know that they are judged on how many of their total dollars they can put toward programs, and they know that donors want to believe that a minimum of their contributions is being used for administration and fundraising. So they find ways, some legitimate and some not, to represent as many of their expenses as programmatic expenses as they can. The social costs of such practices are low for most organizations, and the returns can be counted in accolades about efficiency and the dollars that such accolades bring in" (Hager, 2003, p. 50).

The public no longer accepts these reports alone as valid or credible information. The Internet provides direct access to IRS Form 990 data with other financial details, such as executive compensation, investment returns, and lobbying activities. The Internet also allows easy access to several rating entities acting as self-appointed watchdogs that evaluate nonprofits, assign them scores or grades on their performance, and broadcast their judgments on the Internet (see a list of those who rate nonprofits in Exhibit 6.1). Their main data source is often the IRS Form 990, known to be a flawed report lacking full details with inaccurate figures.

Exhibit 6.1. Raters of nonprofit organizations
Internet Sites
American Institute of Philanthropy, http://www.charitywatch.org
Benefice Information Center, http://www. benefice.com
Better Business Bureau, http://www.give.org
Charitable Choices, http://www.charitablechoices.org/index.htm
Charities Aid Foundation (UK), http://www.cafonline.org

Charities USA, http://www.charitiesusa.com/
Charity Canada, http://www.charity.ca
Charity Guide, http://www.charityguide.org/charity/charityratings.htm
Charity Navigator, http://www.charitynavigator.org
Charity Registration Offices, gopher://people.human.com/00/inc.data/
   states
Copilevitz & Canter, LLC, http://www.exempttaxlaw.com
Give Spot, http://www.givespot.com
GuideStar, http://www.guidestar.org/
Guide to Cruelty Free Giving, http://www/neavs.org/info/charities.
   html
Idealist, http://www.idealist.org
Independent Charities of America, http://www.independentcharities.org
Just Give, http://www/guidestar.org/
Kansas Charity Check, http://kscharitycheck.org
National Association of State Charity Officials, http://nasconet.org
National Commission on Philanthropy and Civic Renewal, http://www.
   ncpcr.org
National Resources Defense Council, http://www.nrdc.org
Society Guardian (UK), http://www.society.guardian.co.uk/charityreform
Wise Giving to Charities, http://www.heartsandminds.org

Media Rating Participants

Chronicle of Philanthropy: Top 400 List, based on amount of money they raise from individuals, foundations, and corporations.

Money Magazine: Selects a few national charities as a benchmark for evaluating other worthy groups. Criteria include devoting a high portion of its income to programs, keeping fundraising costs low, and the organization's A+ rating by the American Institute of Philanthropy.

Nonprofit Times: NPT 100 list, based on amount of funding received from public sources (must be at least 10 percent of total revenue).

Smart Money magazine: Ranks organizations primarily based on how much money they spend on programs but takes into account efficiency in fundraising.

Worth magazine: Lists 100 top charities, based on worthiness of goal and mission, effectiveness of its spending, and its reputation among other nonprofits.

Source: Hart, Greenfield, and Johnston (2005, p. 301).

Unfortunately, these rating groups publish their separate evaluation and measurement scores with often conflicting and contradicting grades given to the same organizations. Furthermore, their arbitrary standards are based on financial indicators alone, adding more confusion than clarity to the value of their services. "Yet, like it or not, charity watchdogs are becoming increasingly popular with the information-hungry public, and the financial ratios they employ are being accepted as proxies for performance, quality and integrity" (Lammers, 2003, p. 34).

Performance evaluations of fundraising results can provide several answers for those responsible for their conduct. Assessments must be able to analyze results with consistency over more than one year to ascertain strengths and weaknesses of the overall fund development effort. Results also should be measured at regular intervals during each fiscal year to make informed decisions, modify current plans, be alert to inadequate returns, identify improvements and act on them, and reallocate the remaining budget for maximum effectiveness and efficiency. This level of performance analysis also will illustrate productivity, profitability, and progress in meeting assigned goals and objectives. The end result will be increased net income for charitable purposes with a bonus: the tools and data needed to forecast future results with reliability.

Accountability for nonprofit health care investments

Health care financial officers, controllers, and business managers can explain a variety of investment strategies, even if they do not use that phrase. They can calculate the point in time when each piece of medical, technical, or mechanical equipment will need replacement, when it has maximized its depreciation value, and when new equipment will begin to show a profit margin based on reimbursement rates, with all mathematical formulas validated in Joint Commission on Accreditation of Healthcare Organizations standards and with a variety of federal, state, and other auditors.

Accountability for financial performance is but a single measurement and fails to show any investment returns on patient programs and services measured against any criteria other than financial. Medicare, Medicaid, health maintenance organizations, physician provider organizations, and other insurers are contract payers who audit patient performance statistics such as diagnosis-related group volumes, length of stay, mortality and morbidity statistics, and more, none of which provide any measurable outcomes on the health of community residents.

Investments in quality assurance methods and continuous quality improvement systems have been introduced into health care organizations. These require participation by boards, administration, medical staff, and employees and have been effective in improving overall medical performance and patient outcomes. They also continue to get better with experience at benchmarking and a staff commitment to dig out the data and do the analysis required. New measurement criteria and tools are being developed that address the effectiveness of management performance along with patient program and service outcomes. This is difficult work due to a multitude of variables relating to the diverse capabilities within organizations, their capacity (structure and process), and their employees' ability (competence and training) to respond and intervene under differing conditions. One preliminary set of accountability guidelines of effectiveness has been identified (Sowa, Selden, and Sandford, 2004, pp. 715–721):

Principle 1: There are multiple dimensions of effectiveness, with the primary dimensions being management and program effectiveness.

Principle 2: Management effectiveness and program effectiveness are further composed of two subdimensions, (a) capacity (processes and structures) and (b) outcomes.

Principle 3: Both objective and perceptual measures are needed to fully capture the dimensions of effectiveness.

Principle 4: A model of organizational effectiveness should allow for organizational and programmatic variations within a systemic structure.

Principle 5: The analytical method used to assess nonprofit organizational effectiveness should capture multiple levels of analysis and model interrelationships between the dimensions of organizational effectiveness.

Active research to identify performance measurement criteria that will demonstrate accountability is being pursued with dedication and commitment across the spectrum of health care providers (see Table 6.1). Patient satisfaction studies provide insights into areas of management effectiveness by using patient satisfaction studies to survey at six-month intervals what patients think about the admission process, food quality and service, complex billing systems, and even parking. In some instances, the intent of these internal assessments has been to arrive at a financial demonstration of budget savings contributing to the overall profitability of the organization. Improving these internal management areas will take time plus financial investments in order to achieve higher satisfaction scores.

A new and perhaps larger concern is the erosion of public confidence and trust in health care organizations, perhaps the bottom line of nonprofit accountability:

So the greatest threat to the not-for-profit sector is the betrayal of public trust, the disappointment of public confidence. Virtually all knowledgeable observers of the not-for-profit scene believe that an overwhelming proportion of not-for-profits are honorably run, even if not most efficiently and effectively. That admirable context, however, does not provide much protection in the sector when a sequence of highly publicized disgraceful not-for-profit misdeeds occurs. Moreover one can be certain that any such occurrences are bound to be highly publicized, because, to

Table 6.1. Nine principles for health care excellence

Principle 1: Commitment to Excellence
Principle 2: Measure the Important Things
Principle 3: Build a Culture Around Service
Principle 4: Create and Develop Leaders
Principle 5: Focus on Employee Satisfaction
Principle 6: Build Individual Accountability
Principle 7: Align Behaviors with Goals and Values
Principle 8: Communicate at All Levels
Principle 9: Recognize and Reward Success

Source: Studer (2003).

do so is the duty—and the glory—of a free press, whose primary function in democratic society is to keep the institutions of society honest by providing the public with information needed to make corrections in existing arrangements. [Fleishman, 1999, pp. 177–178].

Community benefit tests and challenges to tax-exempt privileges are on the rise, due in part to patient complaints and malpractice lawsuits, adding to the loss of public confidence. The search for new revenue streams by governments has targeted the property tax–exempt privilege as a potential source of substantial new tax revenue.

Contributing to concerns of image and reputation is public confusion about the differing performance in health care delivery between for-profit health care providers in competition with nonprofit providers. Concerns over this confusion appear to be shared equally by both for-profit and nonprofit providers and will require management attention along with budget investments in more comprehensive marketing and communications strategies to achieve an unwavering trustworthiness by the public. "In American medicine, concerns about fraud or incompetence are rampant, market policies have been advanced yet many consumers remain ill informed, and accountability has become an increasing focus of contemporary policy debates" (Schlesinger, Mitchell, and Gray, 2004, p. 680). The task ahead is to demonstrate accountability based on a positive investment return for all areas of health care operations measured as greater management effectiveness and patient care efficiency, a tall mountain to climb indeed.

Fundraising budget as an investment strategy

One area for nonprofit accountability focus is the cost of fundraising, a pervasive concern for all nonprofit entities, not just health care organizations. Institutional budgets are subject to stiff competition between priorities for patient care services and administrative necessities, with decisions favoring profit-making departments as a means to pay for unfunded and underfunded programs. As gift, grant, and contribution income is often less than 2 percent of total reimbursement revenue, its forte lies in its application to those operating areas that receive little or no reimbursement funding, such as new programs and services, renovation projects, new construction, and medical research. Fundraising is unique as a reliable profit center within health care administration and often provides greater returns for the budget invested in it than any other department. However, budget and finance officers relegate it as just another cost center competing for scarce annual budget dollars.

Planning a fundraising budget is not a simple transaction, and it is not amenable to analysis by evaluating its results simply by comparing gift revenues with the budget that produced them. Bottom-line measurements may suggest a level of effectiveness and efficiency that is often misleading. Here is a common example. Previously unknown donors include legacies and bequests to the health care organization in their estate plans. Upon receipt, the cash value is reported as new gift income, although no current effort or budget was required to secure the gift and counting it reflects a better bottom-line performance than from active solicitation activities. The misleading presumption is that this same or a greater level of total gift income is possible again, which is unlikely when next year's goals and objectives are set. The fundraising team volunteers and staff are well aware they cannot predict estate gifts from unanticipated and unknown benefactors, and such unrealistic expectations can lead to volunteer resignations and depressed staff morale.

More accurate evaluations and realistic goal setting will come from detailed analysis of the actual performance of each solicitation method, beginning with a focus on the numbers of donors, their individual giving amounts, the method used to solicit their gift, and how they directed their funds to be used. It also is possible to assess the full costs incurred by each solicitation technique, including its proper share of indirect and overhead expenses in the form of back office support.

Indirect and overhead budget allocation and staff time analysis

Each fundraising method contains a full set of office operating costs composed of staff salaries and benefits and administrative expenses required daily for gift processing, record keeping, committee meetings, donor recognition, benefit event planning and preparation, prospect research, and grant writing (see Table 6.2). Indirect and overhead expenses are not easy to allocate between fundraising methods, and it is not an easy task to budget correctly the required day-to-day office expenses for each fundraising activity throughout the year. These support expenses need to be calculated into the cost of preparation, production, and follow-up communications with donors, prospects, and volunteers along with the direct costs of solicitation. It is at this point that the challenge of how to perform joint cost allocation arrives.

One method begins with a time analysis survey performed by all employees. This somewhat unpopular proposal can deliver a reasonably accurate method to estimate staff time spent on direct solicitation activities with related indirect and overhead support to provide labor and nonlabor cost estimates for both (see Exhibit 6.2). Reasonable estimates of indirect costs attributed to each solicitation

Table 6.2. Direct, indirect, and overhead expense areas

Direct costs	Actual expenses to carry out each solicitation method—for example, printing, postage, meetings, space and equipment rentals, food and beverages, entertainer fees, travel expenses, telephone, donor recognition
Indirect costs	Staff salaries and benefits, overtime, meeting support, computer use fees, computer equipment and software, data processing, donor relations and communications, education and training, gift processing and gift reports, Internet access and use fees, newsletters and brochures, office supplies, travel, consultants, purchased services
Overhead costs	Electricity, heat, insurance, rent, water, depreciation assessment

Exhibit 6.2. Worksheet for individual staff time analysis

Group A: Direct Solicitation Activities

(record each activity in 15-minute increments)

Name: _____ Work Week of _____, 20___.

Fundraising Activity	Monday	Tuesday	Wednesday	Thursday	Friday	Other	Totals
Direct mail acquisition							
Direct mail renewal							
Membership club							
Donor clubs							
Phonathons/telethons							
Internet solicitations							
Benefit events							
In memory/in honor gifts							
Volunteer-led solicitations							
Corporate solicitations							
Foundation grant writing							
Individual major gifts							
Special projects							
Capital campaigns							
Planned giving							
Other fundraising activities							
Subtotal:							

Group B: Administration and General Support Activities

Budget preparation
Donor contact
Donor recognition
Education/training
Gift acknowledgments
Gift reports
Meetings (committee)
Meetings (staff)
Personnel activities
Prospect research
Prospect cultivation
Reports/analysis
Newsletter/brochure texts
Volunteer relations
Web site services
Other support activities
    Subtotal:
      Grand total:

activity are derived from the amount of staff time to conduct these solicitations along with all the necessary back office services. Equitable shares of overhead expenses can be allocated based on the office space occupied by each staff member aligned with his or her primary assigned duties corresponding to each solicitation activity. Although this is a somewhat imprecise method, it will provide a fair and equitable allocation of the complete fundraising budget.

Fundraising return on investment and cost-benefit analysis

Money is raised in response to direct solicitation. The results are gifts, grants, and contributions that can be measured and tracked according to each fundraising method used. The first level of analysis adds the budget expenses to solicit this gift income by solicitation method. (See Table 6.3.) A by-product will be the cost-benefit ratio factor for each solicitation method along with overall program productivity figures. What is not measured or shown in this table are any details on how these solicitations performed against other evaluative criteria critical to managing these activities for maximum yield, including: What was the percentage of those solicited who actually gave? What was their average gift size? How many prior donors gave again? How many increased the size of their gift? What was the return on investment for each solicitation method? These data and their evaluations guide the fundraising staff in managing each solicitation's performance and create the data needed to plan for its continued use in the future.

Dollars raised is a firm figure, far easier to pinpoint than the full array of expenses producing this income. To begin to capture these additional costs, all the details surrounding each solicitation method must be tracked. How much gift income was received from each acquisition and each renewal mailing? How many prior donors participated? What was their average gift size? (See Table 6.4.) Numbers of donors are a critical indicator of success; money follows people. This report also illustrates that each solicitation method performs at quite different levels of cost and productivity.

Table 6.3. Income, expenses, and cost-benefit ratio

Solicitation Activities	Gift Income	Budget Expenses	Cost-Benefit Ratio (%)
Annual Giving Programs			
Direct mail (acquisition)	$66,097	$59,795	0.91%
Direct mail (renewal)	84,672	22,150	0.26
Membership club dues	47,150	12,500	0.27
Donor club gifts	124,300	18,900	0.15
Benefit events (net proceeds)	110,865	52,950	0.48
In memorial/in honor gifts	11,452	1,375	0.12
Volunteer-led solicitations	143,750	12,600	0.09
Subtotal:	$588,286	$180,270	0.31%
Major Giving Programs			
Corporations	$31,450	$12,650	0.40%
Foundations	54,000	8,500	0.16
Individuals	476,080	37,600	0.08
Special projects	63,720	13,650	0.21
Capital campaigns	2,177,306	216,500	0.10
Bequests received	168,000	8,500	0.05
Subtotal:	$2,970,556	$297,400	0.10%
Unsolicited gifts	$17,550	$1,000	0.06
Other gifts received	4,950	515	0.10
Subtotal	$22,500	$1,515	0.07%
Grand total:	$3,581,342	$479,185	0.13%
New planned gifts written[a]	$495,000	$116,500	0.23%
Overall productivity	$4,076,342	$595,685	0.15%

[a]Irrevocable agreements for future gifts, part of the annual fundraising budget but not counted as income received. The gift value can be the donor's charitable contribution deduction, fair market value, or net present value based on donor age(s) and life expectancy.

Four additional features remain to be studied, again for each solicitation method in use. (1) Average cost per gift will explain how much fiscal effort was required to realize each gift. (2) Net revenue received is highly important: this is the money for patient care and other mission-driven programs and services of the health care organization. (3) Fundraising cost and (4) return on investment (ROI) will be the bottom-line measurements of overall productivity and profitability (see Table 6.5). In total, these nine points to assess fundraising performance provide a consistent measurement tool for the entire fund development program.

Table 6.4. Individual solicitation program analysis

Solicitation Programs	Gift Income	Number of Donors	Average Gift Size
Annual Giving Programs			
Direct mail (acquisition)	$66,097	1,369	$48
Direct mail (renewal)	84,672	756	112
Membership club dues	47,150	410	115
Donor club gifts	124,300	226	550
Benefit events (net proceeds)	110,865	3	36,955
In memorial/in honor gifts	11,452	409	28
Volunteer-led solicitations	143,750	115	1,250
Subtotal:	$588,286	3,288	$179
Major Giving Programs			
Corporations	$31,450	17	$1,850
Foundations	54,000	12	4,500
Individuals	476,080	88	5,400
Special projects	63,720	216	295
Capital campaigns	2,177,306	891	2,444
Bequests received	168,000	6	28,000
Subtotal:	$2,970,556	1,230	$2,415
Unsolicited gifts	$ 17,550	42	$418
Other gifts received	4,950	16	309
Subtotal	$ 22,500	58	$388
Grand total:	$3,581,342	4,576	$783
New planned gifts written[a]	*$495,000*	*9*	*$55,000*
Overall productivity	$4,076,342	4,585	$889

[a]Irrevocable agreements for future gifts, part of the annual fundraising budget but not counted as income received. Gift value can be the donor's charitable contribution deduction, fair market value, or net present value based on donor age(s) and life expectancy.

Fundraising results are often calculated as a single bottom-line figure focused only on the expense ratio. What should that cost-benefit ratio be? Is $0.20 or $0.25 per dollar raised low enough? What if a budget of $50,000 was invested in a fundraising program and 3,000 donors reply with an average gift of $35.00? This result translates into gross revenue of $150,000 and a net profit of $100,000 with a 200 percent return on investment. Was this an efficient and effective use of budget dollars even if the cost-benefit ratio was $0.33 to raise a dollar? The answer is yes. The true return

Table 6.5. Nine-point performance index

Basic Data	
Number of participants	= Number of donors responding with gifts
Gross revenue	= Value of gifts and contributions received
Expenses	= Fundraising budget
Performance Measurements	
Percentage participation	= Divide participants by total solicitations
Average gift size	= Divide revenue received by participants
Net income	= Subtract expenses from revenue received
Average cost per gift	= Divide expenses by participants
Fundraising cost	= Divide expenses by revenue
Return on investment	= Divide net income by expenses; multiply by 100 for percentage rate of return

Source: Greenfield (1996).

on investment for this effort will be measured in how many of these 3,000 donors give again and where the renewal cost is a fraction of the original acquisition expenses.

Reverse the question about cost-benefit ratio analysis, and study how to measure fundraising results as an investment strategy. If the cost-benefit factor is $0.33, or $0.25, or even $0.20 to raise $1.00, the ROI will be at 200, 290, and 400 percent, respectively, in twelve months or less. Where else can a nonprofit health care organization achieve such impressive financial returns? The issue is not about the math, impressive as it is, but how the fundraising costs were calculated. And ROI percentage offers no details on how the individual solicitation methods performed within their individual reasonable cost parameters (see Table 6.6). These costs vary due to the nonsolicitation costs to support them and the use of volunteers (who work for free, for fun, and for food) to help carry out as much of the work as possible.

Is it expected that fundraising by every nonprofit health care organization will perform at the same level? Will each fundraising method also perform at the same level? The answer is a definite no to both. Cost-benefit ratios alone do not provide accurate assessments of the overall efficiency or effectiveness of the solicitation methods in use. What are the expectations for each and their fit

Table 6.6. Fundraising performance parameters

Solicitation Activity	Reasonable Cost Guidelines
Direct mail (acquisition)	$1.25–$1.50 per $1.00 raised
Direct mail (renewal)	$0.20–$0.25 per $1.00 raised
Membership programs	$0.20–$0.30 per $1.00 raised
Donor clubs	$0.20–$0.30 per $1.00 raised
Benefit events	$0.50 per $1.00 raised (gross revenue and direct costs only)
Volunteer-led solicitations	$0.10–$0.20 per $1.00 raised
Corporate solicitations	$0.20 per $1.00 raised
Foundation solicitations	$0.20 per $1.00 raised
Individual solicitations	$0.10–$0.20 per $1.00 raised
Special project campaigns	$0.10–$0.20 per $1.00 raised
Capital campaigns	$0.10–$0.20 per $1.00 raised
Planned giving programs	$0.20–$0.30 per $1.00 raised

Source: Greenfield (2002, p. 60).

within the overall fund development program's assigned goals to produce the income needed to fund identified priorities? No single measurement tool or bottom-line ratio is available to evaluate overall fundraising performance fairly and equitably.

Multiple factors can influence performance, internal and external, to be considered in any evaluation, including each of the following (Ciconte, 2004, pp. 16–17):

• The age of the organization
• The age of the development department
• The size of an organization
• The profile of the constituency
• The location of the organization
• The popularity of the cause
• The competition for funds

A recent three-year study of administrative and fundraising costs provides evidence of diverse practices among nonprofits due to organization age, size, and mission. The Nonprofit Fundraising and Administrative Cost Project was conducted by the Center on Nonprofit and Philanthropy at the Urban Institute and the Center on Philanthropy at Indiana University. Researchers evaluated management costs of more than 37,500 organizations from their IRS Form 990 reports and surveyed more than 1,500 in detail to gather information about fundraising expenses. Although researchers were not surprised to discover that large organizations spent more on management expenses than small organizations did, they also learned that overall fundraising costs averaged twenty-four cents for every one dollar raised. These costs varied depending on the organization's size, age, and mission. Perhaps most disturbing were the findings that 37 percent of those filing IRS Forms 990 reporting over $50,000 in private contributions also reported no fundraising or special events costs (Hager, Rooney, and Pollak, 2002).

Every nonprofit organization has the means to establish operating standards for its management and fundraising expense using three or more years of its own results. This design is preferred over arbitrary guidelines set by outside organizations and voluntary rating agencies. Furthermore, solicitation programs will mature based on donor and volunteer confidence in the outcomes achieved from their support. A minimum of three years' investment in each solicitation method will be required to achieve consistent returns in the range of reasonable cost parameters.

Fund development is a process and requires time as well as solid effort. Giving is voluntary. Nonprofits must ask often and well, when inviting gifts for clearly identified needs, where their gift income will be used to benefit others. Fundraising is best understood as a business enterprise and a growth industry measured by numbers of participating donors, the quantity of their consistent generosity, and their commitment to maintain their support. If the investments in fundraising can demonstrate a reliable ability to recruit, retain, and upgrade numbers of donors each year, maximum profits from these initial investments will be realized over time, not from counting how much they give each year. A growth-in-giving analysis (see Table 6.7) is a dependable assessment tool to illustrate productivity and profitability and establish a performance standard for future measurement. It also provides a dependable platform to forecast future support in return for added budget investments.

Table 6.7. Growth in giving analysis (overall fundraising program)

	Two Years Ago	Last Year	Annual Rate (%)	This Year	Annual Rate (%)	Cumulative Rate (%)
Participation	1,355	1,605	18	1,799	12	31
Income	$448,765	$507,855	13	$571,235	12	26
Expenses	$116,550	$123,540	6	$131,850	7	13
Participation	39%	44%	13	52%	18	31
Average gift size	$331	$316	–4	$318	–0.4	–4
Net income	$332,215	$384,315	16	$439,385	14	30
Average cost per gift	$86	$77	11	$73	–5	–15
Fundraising cost	$0.26	$0.24	–6	$0.23	–5	–11
Return on expense	285%	311%	9	333%	7	16

Source: Greenfield (2002a, p. 491).

Applications to professional practice

The best use of scarce budget dollars for fundraising ought to be consistent with the organization's goals and objectives beyond fiscal success. Separate from analysis of its donor productivity and investment performance, consider its value as a partner in the organization's communications efforts. Several administrative department budgets are devoted to creating and communicating messages directed to the larger community of past and potential patients and others. Efforts by those responsible for marketing services to patients and broadcasting communications through public information, publications, and media relations often work together to coordinate audiences selected, content, and timing but without collaboration with the fundraising department in its public solicitation messages. It is reasonable to assume that coordination and cooperation will be more effective than each department acting on its own, especially as the audiences intended for these messages are often identical even as the message and its objectives may be different (see Table 6.8). The potential for success in fundraising is directly linked to information given to the public in the form of marketing and communications messages to create legitimacy and credibility for the very patient care programs that funds being raised will provide. It also may be fair to propose that the potential for success by marketing and communications departments depends on favorable public image and reputation as measured by their responses (for example, increased patient volumes, favorable payer mix), further validated by gifts, grants, and contributions from these same audiences.

Program budgeting

Preparation of the annual budget for fundraising begins with program budgeting to estimate the direct costs required to plan and carry out each solicitation activity within the overall fund development program, including the indirect and overhead expenses

Table 6.8. Health care message channels

Marketing message objectives
  Establish an image
  Create clients for programs
  Elicit a positive response
  Stimulate the public to act

Communications message objectives
  Inform and educate
  Tell a story and repeat it often
  Report results, accomplishments, and outcomes
  Build confidence and trust
  Build community consensus

Fundraising message objectives
  Friend raising and relationship building
  Develop a willingness to volunteer
  Develop a willingness to give
  Develop gifts to meet priority needs
  Provide continuous contact with donors

Source: Greenfield (2002b, p. 60).

required to support each activity. Because budgets also are an aid to analysis of their results, a reasonably accurate allocation process is required, program by program, before solicitation begins and the results are counted. Direct costs are more easily identified based in prior years' expense reports. Indirect and overhead costs required as part of each solicitation method are more difficult to assign. One allocation system is to apply the data captured in the staff time analysis worksheet (see Exhibit 6.2). Although perhaps not a perfect model, these data will provide a consistent base for allocating salary and benefits for each staff member plus back office support required for each solicitation method to produce a more complete measurement of return for budget invested.

Health care budget officers require submission of a consolidated annual budget plan that groups together cost estimates for direct expenses, such as mail, printing, postage, telephone, and travel. Fundraising budgets also must include a reasonable allocation of administrative costs to support each solicitation activity. Program budgeting is helpful to monitor expenses during the operating year and for a more accurate cost-benefit analysis of each solicitation activity at fiscal year end. Absent this degree of accounting detail, fundraising programs are subject to a single bottom-line analysis when evaluating their performance based only on total costs compared to total gift revenue. When submitted, fundraising budgets also can reflect anticipated gross revenues as the result of each fundraising method based in prior years' results. Adding budget details and net income along with the cost-benefit ratio and return on investment (see Table 6.9) to illustrate the overall relationship between budget and results can help to educate everyone on the realities of fundraising management.

Each fundraising budget ought to be reviewed against the decisions set as funding priorities, which may or may not match the

Table 6.9. Summary three-year analysis with one-year forecast, including cost of fundraising and return percentages

	Two Years Ago	Last Year	This Year	Estimated Next Year
Gross Revenue				
Direct mail (acquisition)	$27,550	$31,250	$35,500	$42,000
Direct mail (renewal)	66,880	69,500	76,500	85,000
Membership dues	40,400	44,000	48,500	55,00
Benefit events (3)	45,500	53,400	59,600	68,000
Volunteer-led solicitations	58,500	65,500	82,000	92,000
Annual giving total:	$227,830	$263,650	$302,100	$340,000
Corporate giving	$13,500	$28,000	$45,500	$55,000
Foundation giving	8,000	35,500	65,000	80,000
Individual major gifts	35,000	78,000	145,500	160,000
Bequests received	5,000	26,000	45,000	25,000
Major giving total:	$65,100	$167,500	$301,000	$320,000
Gross revenue total:	$289,330	$431,150	$603,100	$660,000
Fundraising Budget				
Direct costs	$ 68,015	$ 72,100	$ 79,778	$ 85,000
Indirect costs	29,550	46,225	51,326	55,000
Subtotal:	$107,565	$118,325	$131,104	$140,000
Net Income	$181,765	$312,825	$471,996	$515,000
Fundraising costs	$0.37	$0.27	$0.22	$0.21
Investment return	169%	354%	360%	367%

Source: Greenfield (1996, p. 277).

giving goals and objectives of donors. Certainly it is important to replace a boiler, build a parking structure, and landscape the grounds. But the donating public wants to support the actual programs and services that are provided directly to benefit patients, such as medical research, new equipment and facilities, indigent patient assistance, and staff education and training. These areas represent for donors where their direct participation is making a difference to the lives of others (even themselves). This information inspires donors to make gifts over and over again, even many times during the same fiscal year.

Budget officers, administrators, and board members seldom review fundraising budgets with any analysis of donor loyalty and retention. Although this is unfortunate, it should be understood that fundraising activities also are devoted to recruiting and retaining donors as friends and concentrating on building these relationships for the benefit of the health care organizations. These efforts are the ties that bind people to their choice of health care organization and, when well attended to, will remain strong long after a series of board members, administrators, and fundraising staff have come and gone from the institution. Recent studies of donor loyalty show that the value of a lifetime relationship with donors is best understood by tracking the numbers of their gifts and cumulative value over many years, not by counting how much they give in any one year (Sargeant and Jay, 2004).

An analysis of donor responses can provide insight into areas of donor preference (see Exhibit 6.3). Giving remains an entirely voluntary response and is more than a one-time experience for most donors. Donors also are willing advocates of improved public health for the community and access to "their" hospital when needed. Donors are a ready pool of potential volunteers who can serve as board members and in other key leadership positions when needed. They also are increasingly generous when they are well informed and personally involved in the organizations they care about.

The annual budget for fundraising is an investment strategy in developing donors who will become a corps of reliable supporters to meet multiple priorities of need, now and in the future, and

Exhibit 6.3. A report on donor giving preferences

Ninety-five percent of all gifts received were restricted in their use.

The predominant donor restrictions were in three areas, representing 85 percent of all gifts received:

Equipment	$2,159,331	48.82%
Education	1,298,142	29.35%
Patient assistance	346,303	07.83%
	$3,803,776	

Gifts for equipment purposes attracted the largest number of gifts: 40 percent of all gifts received. Gifts for education purposes represented 30 percent of all gifts received, and patient assistance received 8 percent. These three donor restrictions total 70 percent of all contributions made and 78 percent of all funds received. The balance (22 percent) was for construction and renovation projects and medical research, with only 5 percent received for unrestricted use.

During the past four years, the Children's Miracle Network program raised more than $1.5 million and confirms a high donor interest and commitment to projects relating to pediatric care.

more than worth the investment and work involved to recruit, renew, and engage them as the organization's partners in fulfilling its mission and vision. Long-lasting relationships built between community residents and their preferred health care organizations are the total return from a fundraising investment strategy. When solicitation techniques are well planned and well executed as a coordinated strategy over several years, they are highly profitable as well as efficient and cost-effective.

Conclusion

The budget invested in fundraising and analysis of its performance is useful for public reports but also valuable to be understood by the nonprofit organization. Many health care organizations operate a comprehensive fund development program led by experienced staff and experienced volunteers who are actively engaged in a variety of solicitations and donors relations. However, nearly all hospitals have formed separate nonprofit foundations as subsidiary organizations to concentrate on fundraising, relieving hospital board members of this added leadership role and management responsibility. This arrangement is productive for fundraising purposes but has led to some distance between the two organizations. Priorities for fundraising are set by the hospital board, and gifts received are spent on patient care programs and services. Annual budget requests for fundraising are ratified by the parent board and included in the consolidated budget proposal.

There is considerable pressure for the budget dollar for internal hospital operations and they deserve the majority of funds available. The fundraising program, by contrast, is engaged in the external world and is not directly responsible for patient cares services, yet is viewed as just another cost center competing for scarce budget dollars. In reality, fundraising is an investment strategy with highly profitable returns. Development staff and volunteers can demonstrate the productivity and profitability of their efforts to produce funds for hospital priorities and should not be reticent to ask for increased budget when they can prove their effectiveness and efficiency. "The reality is that most institutions aren't spending enough on fundraising because their leaders fear public criticism or donor backlash. We need to talk instead about why institutions are underinvesting in themselves. That's the real challenge" (cited in Jaschik, 2005, p. 31).

References

American Institute of Certified Public Accountants. "Statement of Position 98-2, Accounting for Costs of Activities of Not-for-Profit Organizations and State and Local Governmental Entities That Include Fund Raising." New York: American Institute of Certified Public Accountants. Mar. 11, 1998.

American Institute of Certified Public Accountants. *AICPA Audit and Accounting Guide for Health Care Organizations.* New York: American Institute of Certified Public Accountants, May 1, 2004.

Ciconte, B. L. "Calculating Your ROI for Development Costs." *Nonprofit Times,* Nov. 23, 2004, pp. 16–17.

Fleishman, J. L. "Public Trust in Not-for-Profit Organizations and the Need for Regulatory Reform." In C. T. Clotfelter and T. Ehrlich (eds.), *Philanthropy and the Nonprofit Sector in a Changing America.* Bloomington: Indiana University Press, 1999.

Greenfield, J. M. *Fund-Raising Cost Effectiveness: A Self-Assessment Workbook.* New York: Wiley, 1996.

Greenfield, J. M. *Fund Raising Fundamentals: A Guide to Annual Giving for Professionals and Volunteers.* (2nd ed.) New York: Wiley, 2002a.

Greenfield, J. M. *Fund Raising: Evaluating and Managing the Fund Development Process.* (2nd ed.) New York: Wiley, 2002b.

Hager, M. A. "Current Practices in Allocation of Fundraising Expenditures." In M. A. Hager (ed.), *Exploring Measurement and Evaluation Efforts in Fundraising.* New Directions for Philanthropic Fundraising, no. 41. San Francisco: Jossey-Bass, 2003.

Hager, M. A., Rooney, P. M., and Pollak, T. "How Fundraising Is Carried Out in U.S. Nonprofit Organizations." *International Journal of Nonprofit and Voluntary Sector Marketing,* 2002, 7, 311–324.

Hart, T., Greenfield, J. M., and Johnston, M. *Nonprofit Internet Strategies: Best Practices for Marketing, Communications, and Fund Raising Success.* New York: Wiley, 2005.

Jaschik, S. "Price Check." *Currents,* Jan. 2005, p. 31.

Lammers, J. A. "Know Your Ratios? Everyone Else Does." *Nonprofit Quarterly,* Spring 2003, p. 34.

Sargeant, A., and Jay, E. *Building Donor Loyalty: The Fundraiser's Guide to Increasing Lifetime Value.* San Francisco: Jossey-Bass, 2004.

Schlesinger, M., Mitchell, S., and Gray, B. H. "Restoring Public Legitimacy to the Nonprofit Sector: A Survey Experiment Using Descriptions of Nonprofit Ownership." *Nonprofit and Voluntary Sector Quarterly,* 2004, *33,* 673–710.

Sowa, J. E., Selden, S. C., and Sandfort, J. R. "No Longer Unmeasurable? A Multidimensional Integrated Model of Nonprofit Organizational Effectiveness." *Nonprofit and Voluntary Sector Quarterly,* 2004, *33,* 711–728.

Studer, Q. *Hardwiring Excellence: Purpose, Worthwhile Work, Making a Difference.* Gulf Breeze, Fla.: Fire Starter Publishing, 2003.

U.S. Department of Treasury. Internal Revenue Service. "General Instructions for Form 990 and Form 990-EZ." Washington, D.C.: U.S. Government Printing Office, 2004.

JAMES M. GREENFIELD *is president and chief executive officer of JM Greenfield & Associates in Newport Beach, California.*

The process of recruitment for nonprofit institutions is an opportunity for the institution to further define its culture and community, as well as its fundraising goals.

7

Don't fill a position; recruit talent

Gail L. Freeman

LEADERSHIP, TO A GREAT EXTENT, is determined by the needs of the institution. It is more fruitful to consider leadership as a relationship between the leader and the institution than as a universal pattern of characteristics possessed by certain people. Therefore, the effectiveness of recruiting leadership depends on the depth of understanding of the institution's current needs.

There are few decisions as critical as choosing new development leadership for a nonprofit institution. The process of recruitment is an opportunity for the institution to further define its culture and community, as well as its fundraising goals and methodologies. From these defining characteristics, the parameters of the position emerge, and the recruitment strategy is shaped accordingly.

Defining the institution's culture and community

When recruiting talent, it is important to determine the scope or parameters of the position within the institution. The institution should consider the many factors and circumstances that will

NEW DIRECTIONS FOR PHILANTHROPIC FUNDRAISING, NO. 49, FALL 2005 © WILEY PERIODICALS, INC.

influence the scope of the position. Among them are the institution's structure, culture, mission, values, vision, history, staff size, board leadership, administrative leadership, strategic plan, budget, location, sector, fundraising structure, and goals. When recruiting fundraising leadership, the institution should also consider the development history, structure (centralized versus decentralized), volunteer involvement, and short- and long-term fundraising goals.

It is critical to involve stakeholders, both internal and external, in the process of determining these key factors and circumstances. In this way, the stakeholders are automatically engaged in the recruitment process from the beginning stages, which is critical in building consensus and excitement for the new employee. Through interviews, culture and goal assessment, and strategic conversations with key stakeholders, the parameters of the position within the institution become clearly defined and are more easily communicated throughout the recruitment process.

Defining the institution's fundraising goals and methodologies

When recruiting fundraising leadership, such as the director of development, it is compulsory to determine the institution's fundraising goals and methodologies. In defining the institution's current fundraising methodologies, there are many factors to consider: Is the structure centralized or decentralized? Is the development function volunteer or staff driven? What are the fundraising history and levels of support? What are the past and current sources of support (individuals, corporations, foundations, grateful patients, and government)? Is the constituency defined or nondefined? What fundraising vehicles are used to raise support (face-to-face solicitation, grant writing, planned giving, phonathon, special events, direct mail, and e-philanthropy)? What is the development function's budget? What is the current fundraising system? What is the level of expertise and experience on the development team?

Has support been increasing in particular areas, while decreasing in others? What are the fundraising strengths, and, conversely, the weaknesses?

The current fundraising paradigm and the future fundraising goals will have a great impact on the definition and parameters of the director of development. When considering the future fundraising goals, there are many critical areas to define, including the top fundraising priority, the institution's need to diversify its sources of support, the constituency base (is it new, expanding, or established?), an anticipated capital campaign, and the institution's staffing and infrastructural needs to support these goals. The more clearly an institution can define its fundraising goals and methodologies, the more clearly it can determine the skills and experience required for the director of development.

The four pillars: Defining the parameters of the position

It is vital to understand the institution's culture, fundraising history, and future goals when recruiting the director of development. In addition, it is imperative to clearly define the position's four basic dimensions: responsibilities, opportunities, and challenges; qualities and skills needed; important relationships; and compensation. Outlining these four basic dimensions, or pillars, of the search will bolster the institution's ability to recruit the most appropriate candidate.

The main responsibilities, opportunities, and challenges of the director of development are delineated by functional area: supporting the leadership and volunteers, establishing fundraising priorities, and addressing staff management and administration. For fundraising leadership, these parameters are derived directly from the institution's culture, community, and fundraising goals and methodologies. To define the position further, additional strategic questions must be posed: What are the main responsibilities of this position? What opportunities will this individual face? What challenges need to be identified? What are the critical relationships, both internal and external, that need to be forged? What are the short-term and long-term fundraising priorities? Will the director inherit an existing staff or have the opportunity to build a team?

The definition of this first dimension or pillar directly defines the second one of the search: the ideal candidate. The qualities, skills, and experience of the ideal candidate exemplify this pillar. What traits and experiences does the director of development need to be successful? The answer to this question is defined by the position's responsibilities, opportunities, and challenges. Based on these previously defined parameters, the ideal candidate for the director of development must possess certain attributes.

The development professional should have an enthusiasm and passion for the mission of the institution and a depth of understanding of the mission. Since the director of development works with leadership, volunteers, medical staff, grateful patients, and various internal and external constituencies, the ideal candidate must have superlative interpersonal and communication skills. Moreover, this person needs the ability to support and inspire the board and volunteers.

The ideal candidate has to possess a successful track record in all aspects of fundraising, specifically in raising individual, corporate, and foundation support through a variety of vehicles (face-to-face solicitation, direct mail, special events, planned giving, grant writing). Based on the responsibilities, opportunities, and challenges of this position, there may be areas of fundraising expertise that are more relevant to the institution.

It is also important to determine the communication and style best suited for the hospital's culture. Is the environment entrepreneurial or hierarchical? What are the economy of scales? In addition, what are the academic, organizational, cultural, personal, managerial, and administrative qualities needed?

Based on the culture and environment of the institution, the personal qualities desired must be established. Traits and characteristics can include such adjectives as *energetic, entrepreneurial, tenacious, solid, stable, flexible, tactical, strategic, participative, collaborative, team building,* and *self starting.*

Although it can be easy to define the ideal candidate simply by position, this can create a simplistic view that may potentially limit the search and narrow the field of talent. Defining the ideal candidate only by the requirements of the position is natural: "The ideal candidate will have done this exact job in this exact environment." It is critical to analyze a candidate's skill sets in context and not limit the evaluation to a one-dimensional list of experience.

The third pillar or dimension of the position relates to the important relationships, reporting relationships, authority, and span of control. The formal reporting structure should be delineated by direct reporting relationships, including direct manager and direct staff reports. In addition, the areas of oversight and organizational structure should be outlined and illustrated by organizational charts. Visual representations, such as structural organizational charts and functional organizational charts, can be helpful in demonstrating the key relationships and responsibilities of the position.

The fourth dimension or pillar is compensation and budget. The salary range, along with the preliminary budget for the department, should be clearly defined prior to the launch of the active recruitment. Moreover, other compensation should be considered and defined, including relocation costs, signing bonus, and benefits package.

Finally, the position profile is written. This profile is a document that outlines the position's four basic pillars and includes a brief history of the organization and other pertinent background and historical information necessary for a candidate to develop a clear understanding of an institution and its mission. The profile also provides a snapshot of the institution's current achievements and visions for the future.

Designing the recruitment strategy

Once the position is defined and the profile prepared, the institution is poised to design and implement the recruitment strategy.

First, the institution has the choice of conducting an internally driven search or retaining outside search counsel. Many factors influence this decision, including budget, position level, location, and previous experience.

Second, the institution should define what makes this opportunity unique. It needs to decide how to attract the best candidates for the position. Is it a special opportunity because of the institution's reputation, its fundraising initiatives, or notable leadership? This appraisal determines the advertising and outreach strategy needed to find the ideal candidate.

Advertising serves many purposes in the recruitment process. Beyond the obvious recruitment function, strategic advertising can help to promote the institution's goals and public relations by illuminating positive change and exciting initiatives. Today there are many viable varieties of advertising, including print advertising, Internet advertising, and targeted mailings.

Internet advertising is typically less expensive than print advertising. Despite its convenience and lower cost, Internet advertising should be carefully considered. Due to the ease of Internet applications, haphazardly placing advertisements on Internet job sites may result in an overwhelming number of unqualified applications. A hospital placing a director of development advertisement with the Association of Healthcare Philanthropy is likely to have a better response than placing the advertisement on a generalist job site such as Monster.com.

An additional option for advertising is targeted mailings, in both hard copy and electronic forms. For example, a hospital may be a member of the Association of Healthcare Philanthropy and have several contacts with other member institutions. Distributing a job announcement to these contacts in a targeted fashion can result in candidates, as well as garner helpful advice and suggestions from peer institutions and colleagues.

The recruitment process can be active or passive. Some institutions may choose to limit the search outreach to advertisements. This passive strategy allows applicants to approach the institution directly. Alternatively, the institution can pursue an active outreach for potential candidates. In this situation, the institution may assign staff or partner with outside search counsel to strategically contact likely candidates in similar institutions in size, mission, and scope of responsibility. Typically, active outreach is combined with strategic advertisement. Actively networking for potential candidates requires more resources than passive applications, but the results can be dramatically different.

Once the recruitment process has been determined, the institution needs to define the process for application management and candidate identification and development. Application management, as mundane as it might seem, plays an important role in the public appearance and results of the recruitment. If the application process is not well organized, it can result in the untimely response, acknowledgment, and review of résumés. This oversight can lead to the institution's appearing disorganized and unprofessional to candidates. Therefore, it is valuable to properly set up and provide support to the application process.

Candidate identification and development

Once launched, the recruitment strategy results in applications for the position. Next steps include résumé review, telephone interviews, face-to-face interviews, group interviews, candidate management, and reference checking.

All résumés should be reviewed and evaluated on several factors, including tenures, institutions, education, and management. The cover letter and résumé organization and preparation should be considered an illustration of the applicant's ability to effectively communicate his or her skills, abilities, and professional experience. Résumés should be reviewed with the position profile in mind, with special focus on the qualities and experience of the ideal candidate. In addition, the effectiveness of the résumé to portray these attributes should be taken into serious consideration.

Applicants whose listed experience seems to be an appropriate match to the position should be contacted by telephone. This initial contact allows the institution's representative to evaluate the applicant's style and potential fit within the institution.

Based on the initial telephone conversation, likely candidates should be interviewed in person by key representatives of the institution. The stages of face-to-face interviews depend on many factors, including time line, institution procedures, parties involved, and human resource requirements. Often the applicant first meets with his or her potential direct supervisor. This initial interview should be used to delve into the applicant's experience, skill set, personal characteristics, and style. It also allows the interviewer to judge the applicant's demeanor and potential fit within the institution's culture and environment.

The next stage of interviews can take many forms, including group or search committee interviews, additional one-on-one interviews, or a combination of the two. The number of interviews and types of interviews depend on the institution and its goals and procedures. Just as a candidate prepares for interviews with the institution, the institution's representatives should prepare for the candidate interviews, specifically by conducting in-depth résumé review, interview question preparation, and crafting hypothetical scenarios for the interviewer to pose to each candidate.

Regardless of the institution's interview process, it is important to underscore the critical nature of candidate management. When candidates are engaged in a recruitment process, it is critical for the institution's representatives to communicate effectively and consistently to the candidates in a timely manner. For example, if a candidate is interviewed by a search committee, it is vital for the institution to follow up with the candidate to ascertain his or her feedback and answer any questions, as well as share feedback and next steps. A candidate who is not contacted in a timely manner may interpret the inaction as a lack of interest or a lack of professionalism on the part of the institution.

Based on the outcome of the interview process, the final candidates are selected. The institution, in collaboration with its human resource or personnel department, should conduct in-depth reference checks on the selected candidates. In essence, reference checks are a second opinion: they provide reassurance that the qualities and experiences of the final candidates are true.

Evaluating talent and fit

During the interview process, it is vital to consider the candidates in the context of the institution's culture, fundraising history, and future goals. To this end, it is imperative to evaluate the candidates clearly based on the four pillars of the position.

The interview process is essential in identifying, evaluating, developing, and recruiting the best candidates. During the interview process, it is important for the interviewer to set the tone, whether formal, informal, or informational, and develop a relationship with each candidate. The interviewer should present an overview of the institution, the position's role in the institution, and current institutional priorities.

During the interview, it is effective to focus on the four pillars of the position. There are many effective, strategic questions to ask. For a director of development interview, examples may include the following: Why do you have a passion for this mission? What in your background and experience makes you feel that you are qualified for this position? How and why did you enter the fundraising field? Can you tell me your career story?

The interview process is also the candidate development process. This is the institution's chance to market the position and recruit the candidates. Incorporating a facility tour, basic orientation, and benefits review can all be helpful in recruiting. Depending on the institution's time line and procedures, final candidates may meet with potential staff.

The institution should evaluate the final candidates on several criteria including experience, presentation, and potential fit.

During the selection process, the institution should consider the four pillars of the position. It is critical to understand and accept that there is no perfect candidate. The institution should rank candidates based on their experience and set criteria. However, it is vital that candidates be rated on intangible criteria, specifically, fit and chemistry within the institutional framework. The best skill set cannot overcome a bad cultural fit.

Closing the search

After an extensive interview and recruitment process, the final candidate is selected. The preparation and negotiation of the offer should be viewed as an extension of the recruitment, not a separate action. How the offer is made can determine the outcome of the negotiation. For example, if the president of the hospital personally extends an offer to the final candidate for the director of development position, it has a direct impact on the candidate's interpretation of the situation and offer. If a human resource representative makes the same offer, the candidate can interpret and react differently. If procedure dictates that human resources must extend the offer, it would be strategic to engage a key stakeholder, such as the president, to extend a preliminary offer to the candidate. The offer should include compensation and other benefits, as well as the start date.

With the offer accepted, the institution should close the search with the same care and strategy used throughout the search process. As in application management, the institution's procedure in closing and announcing the placement directly reflects on its public image. The institution should first notify and thank any other final candidates that the search has been successfully completed. Beyond personal courtesy, this action may assist the institution in future recruitments and outreach. The successful placement should also be announced publicly. The position level, resources, and timing will determine the location and extent of the public announcement. At a minimum, the institution's internal and external communications, such as a newsletter or Web site, should list the announcement.

Once the new team member is on board, it is essential to set clear expectations and benchmarks. And it can be helpful to provide mentors within the institution to offer insight into the best ways to navigate, interact, and communicate with internal and external constituencies.

The following lists serve as a summaries of the search process and as checklists for both the institution and the candidate.

Search Checklist for Institutions

1. Getting it together: Crafting an organizational chart.
2. Don't leave them guessing: Providing a list of expectations.
3. Where's the money? Presenting a comprehensive budget.
4. How much have you got? Giving the total fundraising dollars raised to date.
5. Who are you? Collating and compiling collateral materials.
6. How do you raise your money? Explaining the fundraising methodology.
7. Capital campaign experience.

Search Checklist for Candidates

1. Who are you? Developing a comprehensive résumé.
2. Check me out: Compiling and contacting professional references.
3. Just one look: First impressions mean everything.
4. Getting to know you: Do your due diligence.
5. Hello, it's me: Sell yourself and not the field.

There are few decisions as critical as choosing new development leadership for a nonprofit institution. The process of recruitment is an opportunity for the institution to further define its cultural, community, and fundraising goals and methodologies.

GAIL L. FREEMAN *is president of Freeman Philanthropic Services LLC in New York City.*

The fundraising profession has grown dramatically over four decades. It is now more important than ever before to attract and keep top talent.

8

Attracting top talent and retaining stars

Claudia A. Looney, James K. Looney

WHEN SEEKING TO HIRE candidates, you must address and answer key questions related to attracting top talent. Why would a good candidate look at your open position? At the top of the list are the reputation of the organization and the reputation of the leadership. Salary and benefits must be competitive, but top talent follows the top leadership who has a vision for the future of the organization and a proven track record of success in achieving goals.

Many questions and issues come into play in recruiting top talent. You have goals in mind, as does the candidate. You want to understand what the candidate is looking to achieve with a career move. Asking strategic questions to get to the root of these motivations will help you determine if the candidate is a good fit for the position and will demonstrate to the candidate that you are interested in him or her.

It is more than likely your candidates will not have the years and depth of experience that you are seeking. Dee Hock, the founder and CEO emeritus of VISA, suggests the following: "Hire and promote first on the basis of integrity; second, motivation; third, capacity; fourth, understanding; fifth, knowledge; and last and least,

NEW DIRECTIONS FOR PHILANTHROPIC FUNDRAISING, NO. 49, FALL 2005 © WILEY PERIODICALS, INC.

experience. Without integrity, motivation is dangerous; without motivation, capacity is impotent; without capacity, understanding is limited; without understanding, knowledge is meaningless; without knowledge, experience is blind. Experience is easy to provide and quickly put to good use by people with all the other qualities" (Waldrop, 1996, p. 79).

If you believe that candidates with experience and knowledge are limited, then the task at hand of attracting the best candidates is even more crucial. The answers and success depend on your organization. What will capture the top candidates' attention?

An organization with a compelling mission that resonates with the candidate is key. You may believe that your mission is pure and extraordinarily important. But if the candidate does not strongly and unflinchingly align with your organization, the candidate is not right one. The mission of the organization is also clearly linked to its strategic vision. What are the exciting and visionary goals for the organization that will empower fundraising? The excitement of the vision is at the core of attracting the best candidate. If the organization does not have a strategic plan or a vision and is interested only in maintaining the status quo, then the likelihood of attracting top candidates is limited.

Beyond the vision, top candidates will probe whether the infrastructure is in place. Is there a sufficient budget to support the fundraising function? Will the administrative and board leadership support fundraising? Is the board engaged in the fundraising process?

The top candidates will want to know if the communication avenues open to them are linked to the strategic vision for the organization. They will want to be able to influence, motivate, and inspire those decision makers. Without that sense of empowerment, the top candidates will turn away from seeking a position with your organization.

The fit with the culture of the organization is essential. As an example, a professional fundraiser may be enthralled with the organization's mission, but the politics and complexity of the organization may make it difficult for a fundraiser who does not like to be challenged or does not have the capacity to deal with ambiguity. This example does not advocate conformity or similarity, but suggests that the skills and style that are needed for the organization are important considerations for candidates and for the organization. The candidate needs to fill a void in the organization. A fundraiser may be the person who is needed at that time to organize the fundraising function or to complete a capital campaign, but if the anxiety grows each day for the fundraiser, the fit is probably not right for the long term.

Fit also extends to the interpersonal skills of looking at the situation from the perspective of others. The candidates will want to know if they have access to the calendar of the president or CEO. They will want to understand the pace and timing of the organization. Is that pace a good fit? The candidates will want know if the organization allows honest feedback. The integrity of the organization will be a key element in the recruitment.

Most of all, the reputation of the organization for doing good work will be paramount to top candidates. Each will want to know if the organization will be better off if he or she joins the fundraising team. Most of the top candidates will come to the table with a reputation for results. They will expect the same from you and your organization.

Finding top talent

These issues are at the heart of why so many institutions turn to an executive search to find likely candidates. The cost of hiring a search firm is measured against the time you take away from fundraising by doing the search internally. More than likely, your organization's human resource department is not focused on fundraising searches. If your organization is a hospital, for instance, the human resource department will be consumed with hiring nurses and medical technologists. Fundraising staff are positioned behind the patient care–related vacancies. In addition, it is simply not the human resource department's expertise. For the most part, that leaves the recruitment up to the development officer.

The first task in initiating a search is to take a look internally for candidates to promote. You may not believe that someone already on staff is experienced enough to take on the enhanced responsibilities, but you may lose that valuable fundraiser by overlooking her or him. You might ask yourself if you would be greatly disappointed if that person you have not promoted is recruited away. If you would, you might remember the words of Hock and recall that knowledge and experience take a second chair to other skill sets.

The next step is to look to your network of colleagues. Methodically set about developing a list of all those whose opinion you value and whose reach extends beyond yours. You ask them who they believe is capable of doing the position you have open. It is not about who is looking for a position. Call your colleagues across the nation to see if they know of anyone who is seeking to move to another state because of family or health issues with an aging parent. It is becoming common among seasoned fundraisers that they are now expected to manage their parents' health and are desirous of being closer to them. Professional fundraising organizations are another good source. Each office has job postings locally and nationally. Being aggressive and posting the positions on more than one occasion with professional organizations might be worth the time and expense.

Succession planning

Often the best and most qualified candidates for positions in the development office are already employed by the office in a variety of capacities. However, these employees frequently do not see that there is interest in developing their skills and promoting from within, and there is not active succession planning by the organization.

Even a small development office can have a rudimentary succession planning activity; larger offices will have more complex and frequently updated plans. Figure 8.1 is a useful tool in thinking about candidates for currently filled positions. These charts are maintained confidentially, of course, but they do provide an opportunity to consider the possibility that incumbents may leave and offer the opportunity to lay plans in a proactive manner. If internal candidates are

Figure 8.1. Succession planning chart

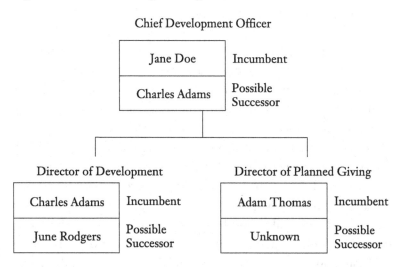

Chief Development Officer

| Jane Doe | Incumbent |
| Charles Adams | Possible Successor |

Director of Development

| Charles Adams | Incumbent |
| June Rodgers | Possible Successor |

Director of Planned Giving

| Adam Thomas | Incumbent |
| Unknown | Possible Successor |

identified, training programs and other activities can be undertaken to prepare them for promotion. The fact that a development office has demonstrated interest in promoting from within will have a salutary effect on the morale of the office in general.

Retaining the stars

In 2000, Carole J. Gilbert, the managing director of Korn/Ferry International, conducted a fund development survey. She discovered that the top fundraisers were being called twice monthly by executive recruiters. She also noted that "what appears to keep most of you in your current positions is generally the mission of your organization and its reputation" (C. J. Gilbert, letter to C. Looney, Oct. 10, 2000).

Pride in your organization and pride in the quality of the fundraising for your institution will make it more difficult for a fundraiser to say yes when the phone call eventually comes from an executive recruiter. If the fundraiser feels respected, has been given ownership of his or her work, and is supported with the resources to do the job, then that person's pride will become apparent.

Trust, respect, and ethical behavior by the leadership in all transactions are core values that will retain the stars. Being generous with praise and compliments creates pride, enhances enthusiasm, and energizes the professional for taking on the tasks at hand. The commitment of the leadership to empower colleagues and position them for success will also make it less appealing to leave.

Turnover will happen even in the best organizations with strong missions and outstanding reputations. Small development offices cannot provide career paths. Often, small development offices are not able to provide competitive salaries or appealing compensation packages. There will always be organizations that will offer more money. Mission, reputation, and respect for your organization's leadership however, will make top candidates think carefully about moving to a new job.

If your organization has a CEO and board who understands the importance of philanthropy, you have something to offer that many others cannot provide. Spending time to address engagement issues related to the leadership and the board will pay off when it comes to recruitment and retention. A strong culture of philanthropy, a solid fundraising track record, successful colleagues to work beside, a collaborative management team, and vibrant and challenging goals will also attract and retain top performers.

A good work environment is essential since employees often spend more hours at work than at home. Creating a place where employees want to be needs constant attention. It may seem simple but knowing what is expected and making certain that top performers have working equipment (computers, cell phones, printers, faxes) make or break job satisfaction. Regular and heartfelt recognition and praise for their work are paramount as well.

Creative opportunities to learn and grow on the job encourage retention. Providing opportunities for increasing a fundraiser's knowledge base, networking with colleagues, and attending conferences and seminars demonstrates commitment to professional growth and allows learning and career development.

Our experiences suggest that leadership and management must not only set the tone for the organization, but must enthusiastically share the vision. Keeping the mission close and personal with each fundraiser takes time and energy. It is our observation that creating strategies for involving staff early in the planning phase of a project and empowering them with ownership for implementation is energizing and encourages attachment to the organization.

Continuing with personal attention as the project unfolds by supporting the fundraiser with encouragement, learning opportunities, and praise works well. Alternatively, assisting the fundraiser who is in need of help is balanced by allowing opportunities to take risks, fail, and rebound. Leaders must learn how to treat failures as learning experiences. Leaders should also be alert to other signs of disengagement, including stress, not allotting enough time to complete projects, inaccessibility to leadership, and complex and highly charged political environments that create anxiety and lead to the willingness of fundraising stars to look elsewhere for employment.

Development offices in diverse communities are faced with the fact that the future population of donors increasingly differs from the ethnicity of the development staff. The number of African American, Latino, and Asian fundraisers is not great, even in the most diverse communities. To deal with this issue effectively, development offices will have to consider creative solutions. Internship programs in cooperation with a local college or university that allow interns to explore fundraising as a career is a solution to two issues: it will potentially create a larger pool of minority candidates, and it will create a pool of individuals for vacancies in the sponsoring organization. It is important, however, to realize the magnitude of the undertaking: internship programs require attention to curriculum development and to ongoing and helpful supervision of the interns if success is to be achieved.

The strategies related to recruitment and retention have much in common. Mission-driven organizations that are focused on visionary priorities will attract more potential candidates and keep the fundraising stars engaged with the organization. Individuals you want to keep and those you hope to attract need to be able to handle the fast pace of a high-performing fundraising operation.

The fundraising process, goals, and strategies of high-performing organizations evolve and change as rapidly as in businesses for profit. Change and dealing with ambiguity are traits that are useful and encouraged. Knowledge of fundraising and demonstrated skills in securing gifts are valuable in the world where three to five years of experience as a fundraiser is seen as "seasoned."

Clearly recruitment and retention are complex and varied. Yet the most important consideration may be the simplest concept of all: the fundraising star enjoys the work. When there are so many choices for fundraisers and a constant desire to achieve work-life balance, having fun will make all the difference in attracting the stars and retaining top talent. After all, we spend too much time at work not to enjoy what we are doing.

Economics of health care development jobs

In developing actions and policies that attract and retain high-quality development staff, the impact of supply and demand and the economics of compensation are often not addressed as aggressively as they might be.

Institutions that employ development staff need to recognize that the development job market has its own characteristics that dictate whether an institution can compete successfully for staff and eventually retain them. Currently, the demand for highly productive development officers vastly exceeds the supply. To attract and retain the most competent staff in this environment means that in addition to the many cultural and management issues discussed in this chapter, the economics of compensation must receive significant attention.

The chief development officer should develop a close working relationship with the chief of human resources and provide that person with information about the state of the development marketplace. The human resource department should be encouraged to do frequent salary surveys for comparable development positions in institutions with which your office is competitive for talent. It is important to understand if you intend to hire primarily locally or regionally or are in a national market for each position in the organization. It is equally important to understand which institutions tend to set the competitive salary markets for your area.

Turnover in development offices is frequently caused by the abundance of opportunities at higher salary levels at other institutions. If your institution applies absolute caps to salary increases, it will be increasingly difficult to reward highly productive development officers and retain them for the organization. Health care institutions have generally been much more open to consideration of bonus and other compensation plans to reward high performers. This recognition of differential performance is crucial to attracting candidates (outstanding performers will want to know they will be in this kind of environment) and retaining them (they will be rewarded for outstanding performance). Another effective tool is the retention or tenure bonus: key individuals may be offered a one-time bonus for meeting performance objectives and staying for a specified period of time—five years, or to the completion of a campaign, for example.

Attracting and retaining the top talent for your office will require close cooperation with the human resource office, the CEO of the institution, and the board, and the creation of salary structures and reward systems that recognize top performance and assist you in retaining your key individuals.

Reference

Waldrop, M. W. "Dee Hock's Management Principles, in His Own Words." *Fast Company*, Oct.–Nov. 1996, p. 79.

CLAUDIA A. LOONEY *is senior vice president of development at Childrens Hospital Los Angeles in Los Angeles.*

JAMES K. LOONEY *is senior vice president and managing director of Grenzebach Glier & Associates in Chicago.*

Benchmarking should not be viewed as a number or a goal to be achieved. The value of benchmarking is its use as a management tool to improve fundraising performance.

9

Performance benchmarking: Lessons on using performance benchmarks to maximize fundraising results

Stuart R. Smith

BENCHMARKING is a term too often viewed as a number or thought of as a goal to be achieved. The most common use is often simply stated as a cost-benefit ratio that should be achieved to reflect a good fundraising program. "It should cost no more than twenty cents to raise one dollar"—or something similar to that statement—is often the challenge given to the fundraising management team. Unfortunately, although that ratio sounds reasonable, it does not exist, just as "average gift" is nowhere to be found in pragmatic terms. At best, it is a calculation often made from data reported by many. Outcomes vary widely due to a wide range of methodologies and specifications under different definitions and guidelines.

National benchmarking collaboration

In 2003, a group of twelve health care chief development officers united to create a process for more effective and more reliable

NEW DIRECTIONS FOR PHILANTHROPIC FUNDRAISING, NO. 49, FALL 2005 © WILEY PERIODICALS, INC.

performance benchmarking (Table 9.1). Performance benchmarking establishes a measurement process to provide management with information to allocate human resources and program capital to maximize fundraising productivity. It also provides information to help measure activity on a routine basis, which enables efficiencies and timely corrections for achievement of these benchmarks.

Under this definition, performance benchmarking is seen as a management tool instead of a judgmental tool that establishes a passing or failing performance. Although the latter is valuable, it is a view of the past. If it shows failure to achieve goals, then outcomes are often reduced to future investment, which actually prevents recovery or turn-around.

The new view of performance benchmarking was defined along three objectives by the group of twelve:

1. What is the best measurement of fundraising productivity over a given time frame?
2. What is the best methodology to track performance?
3. What information can be tracked monthly to reflect progress and enable adjustments to maximize achievement of these annual outcomes?

Table 9.1. Collaboration of Health Care Foundations and Resource Development Programs: Participants

Ken Holden, Baylor Health Care System Foundation
Gene Attal, Seton Fund, Seton Healthcare Network
John W. Bozard, Orlando Regional Healthcare Foundation
Ken Kirby, Main Line Health
Gay Clark, INTEGRIS Health Foundations
Susan Ell, Advocate Charitable Foundation
Frank R. Hall, St. Joseph Health System
Allen Peckham, Partners HealthCare System
Paulette Roberts, Affiliated Foundations, Meridian Health
Linda Kay Smith, HealthEast Foundation
Stuart R. Smith, Banner Health Foundation
Steve Meyerson, Inova Health System Foundation

The immediate realization was that although each of the twelve organizations formally tracked and accounted for their respective fundraising activity, the language and categories for collection differed. Thus, the goal of creating any benchmark demanded that common rules and reporting be enforced, regardless of each organization's existing requirements.

A measurement goal was set to build a predictive tool in an effort to secure the support of the operations managers within the hospital setting. It was designed much like a hospital operating department or service line. For instance, if Hospital A's obstetrics unit is expected to deliver a thousand births in the year's plan, the components to achieve that number must be monitored. If the highest-performing obstetrics practice left the institution in midyear, the manager would immediately know that specific actions could be implemented to offset that loss, such as decreasing inventory, adjusting staff, increasing marketing, and implementing a recruiting strategy to replace the group that left. This monthly performance tracking is valuable and necessary to drive both the year-end objectives and measure ongoing activity against opportunity.

Traditional thinking has focused on measuring outcomes, not processes. All too frequently, successful fundraising was expressed in the statement that was predicated on a belief that it should cost twenty cents to raise one dollar. That simple observation simplistically drives organizational thinking to choose cost reduction rather than to provide more resources for more productive activity, which would drive up revenue and change the ratio to a more favorable number.

To address this, the collaborating group established a series of benchmarks to calculate outcomes, creating tracking guidelines to help systems measure progress toward those outcomes. Agreement was achieved on the use of two annual outcome measurements: one reflecting funds collected and the other total fundraising production (Table 9.2).

To achieve this collective purpose, a common glossary of terms was agreed on that enabled accurate collection and comparison.

Table 9.2. Benchmark indicators sample

Benchmark	Definition	Rationale
	DASHBOARD INDICATORS (BOARD MONITOR)	
Cost to raise $1 cash	The product achieved by dividing gross cash by dollars spentraising the funds	What the board looks at as an indicator of money available to the hospital
1. Annual gifts of less than $10,000, including memorial gifts	Salaries and Benefits:	
2. Current major gifts ($10,000 and over), corporate gifts, and foundation gifts, including memorials	Executive Positions (System and Unit) -Chief Development Officer -Directors of Development	
3. Payments on pledges, letters of intent, and other monies promised over a period longer than a fiscal year	Function (System and Unit) Personnel primarily responsible for the following: -Major Gifts -Annual Gifts -Planned Gifts -Special Events	
4. Planned gift maturities and bequests from decedents' estates		
5. Charitable gift annuity agreements (whether current or deferred) at a value equal to the donor's allowable charitable contribution deduction for the gift	-Campaign Specialists (e.g., grant writing [except public support], foundation relations, etc.) -Prospect research -Writing/Public Relations/Marketing -Gift receipting	
6. Net event income including sponsorships and event underwriting	Purchased Services/Professional Fees: Rent/Occupancy	

Supplies

Travel/Dues/Subscriptions

Other: cultivation expenses, gifts, recognition, etc.

The product achieved by dividing total funds actually raised (not just collected) and gift commitments made in the year by total dollars spent raising the funds

This is what is actually produced as a result of the investment for the year

Cost to raise $1 of production

1. Annual gifts of less than $10,000 including memorial gifts
2. Current major gifts ($10,000 and over), corporate gifts and foundation gifts (that were not payments on prior year pledges)
3. The full value of pledges, letters of intent, and other monies promised over a period longer than a fiscal year
4. New planned gift commitments, with the exception of charitable gift annuity agreements, at their face value
5. Charitable gift annuity agreements at a value equal to the donor's allowable charitable contribution deduction for the gift
6. Net event income including sponsorships and event underwriting

Source: Collaboration of Health Care Foundations and Resource Development Programs, 2003. This work was guided by Growth Design Corporation, Milwaukee, Wisconsin.

Initially, it was recognized that the twelve participating groups accounted for information in different, but allowable, methodologies within their own operating and reporting environments. Therefore, common ground was critical to the group. Again, this was done not so much for a sense of absolute numbers but rather for important tracking of resource allocation, viewing outcomes, and enabling discovery of common or best practices within the better-performing organizations.

In the macro view, when comparing funds collected versus production, it became evident that the outcomes achieved in each area were important and would ebb and peak depending on investment and program life cycle. In other words, the best evaluation of the cost-benefit ratio is reflected in two measurements over three to five years. Funds collected against costs of program investment would reflect either higher outcomes or lower cost as time elapsed over a five-year period, and just the opposite would occur for production.

A simple example to demonstrate this cost-benefit ratio is a five-year capital campaign that requires high early investment for early leadership gifts and start-up activity. Early production of gifts is high while gift collection is low. As new pledges decrease in size and totals and collections increase, the cost-benefit reported in funds collected versus funds produced is reversed. It is only when the five-year average of each is viewed in that context that there is better understanding of the cost-benefit ratio and longitudinal performance. Benchmarking the five-year program performance brings greater meaning when compared against others within the same collaborative group (those who have accounted for their data in the same fashion).

Restated, in the first year, it is possible to have a cost of funds collected in the forty-cent range to produce one dollar and a cost of funds produced to be fifteen cents to raise one dollar. In the fifth year, that ratio could be expected to reverse if management chooses to reinvest in highly productive efforts and launches a new campaign or major gift initiative. The funds invested never decrease, but instead rise as inflation, environmental factors (community growth and increased demand, for example), and productivity gains are realized. Performance benchmarking should forecast that certain fundraising service lines can raise production by adopting best practices.

Having established the macro view of performance benchmarking for production and collection, the collaborators investigated a micro view or "best practice" activity by service line. Performance benchmarking achieves its best use in the micro view once the organization sets its overall annual and five-year expectation. Monthly monitoring of program activity then produces the year-end outcomes.

These measurements again were arbitrary at first but were subsequently agreed on by the collaborative group leading the study. To dive into fundraising service lines, the major gifts category was selected as the first and most productive service line, offering the best common understanding and practice within the collaboration. Prospect portfolio management under the direction of a major gift officer was selected as the model.

Similar performance benchmarks were also established by the group for planned giving, annual giving, and special event service lines along common practices. Table 9.3 details the data for performance benchmarks needed to track the major gift activity.

Addressing only the major gift service line as an example, the activity measured for each major gift officer is tracked monthly. Each major gift officer is expected to manage a portfolio of 120 prospects over a year's activity, and his or her performance is tracked monthly. This is done by formal reporting of contact activity (cultivation) and frequent evaluation by management, often in a team setting, to share best practices and coordinate efforts for maximum outcomes. The agreed-on goal of eighty actively engaged prospects per year requires precise donor prospect cultivation, weekly engagement, and a thorough working knowledge of those donor prospects who will move toward making a gift during the course of a twelve-month relationship-building process.

Similar to the hospital operating officer in the earlier example who is charged to meet a thousand births within the obstetrics department, if a potential donor for a major gift relocates in July,

Table 9.3. Major gifts performance benchmarks
Dashboard Indicators

Percentage of major gifts officers and corporate fundraisers on staff	Proportion of major gifts fundraisers in relation to the total staff	Speaks to the resources of the department and its capacity to raise major gifts
Number of prospects	Total number of major gift prospects assigned to each major gift officer: Benchmark Goal: 120 prospects	Speaks to prospect assignments of field staff
Number of visits	Total number of personal solicitation visits to major gift, corporate, and foundation prospects: Benchmark Goal: 80 actively being cultivated	Speaks to activity level of field staff
Number of proposals delivered for gifts of $10,000 or more (major gift amount)	Total number of formal written proposals submitted for major gifts (gifts equal to or more than $10,000): Benchmark Goal: 40	Indicates level of qualified activity
Number of gifts of $10,000 or more	Total number of major gifts secured (gifts that are equal to or more than $10,000 in value) in response to proposal delivered: Benchmark Goal: 20	Indicates quality of proposals delivered Indicates effectiveness of planned gifts

Source: Collaboration of Health Care Foundations and Resource Development Programs, 2003. This work was guided by Growth Design Corporation, Milwaukee, Wisconsin.

then that major gift officer recognizes immediately that new activity must be initiated to identify and cultivate a new relationship if he or she hopes to achieve the existing targets (benchmarks) for year-end success. This kind of performance benchmarking creates a real sense of urgency and energetic focus in July, long before the traditional year-end push. And so tracking the performance benchmarking continues through the submission of forty formal solicitation proposals with the expectation of twenty positive responses.

The continual reporting of this process forces ongoing performance in each measurement because major gift officers are constantly maintaining activity that is formally documented and reviewed monthly by internal managers. The result is that the traditional rush and focus of year-end requests now becomes a monthly performance check, a much more predictable and productive action plan.

Another distinct advantage of maintaining frequent dialogue between major gift officers and the overall major gift service line manager is stronger team interaction. This leads to more effective information sharing within the development team and, equally important, is conducive to forming a multiple layer of involvement for all concerned in this process.

Sharing reports and monitoring collective development activities, whatever the size, essentially encourages each team member to have both a higher stake and a focused ownership in the overall team's success. Furthermore, this multilayered approach provides every major gift officer with the opportunity to offer recommendations on remedial action or to pose measures that are needed for goal achievement. Over the long run, this technique ensures that individual and team success become more achievable from year to year, which is clearly a beneficial methodology.

Collaborative lessons

Early lessons emerging from these collaborative efforts demonstrate that fundraising organizations should consider aligning human and capital resources in business lines for performance benchmarking. The overly simplified belief that more funds can be raised while the annual commitment to budget can be decreased is now seen as foolish thinking. Nothing demonstrates the flaws in this thinking more than the expectation that last year's bequest can be automatically increased the following year. Bequests are

Figure 9.1. Performance indicators

PHILANTHROPY
RESOURCES
Professional staffing
Fundraising budget

EDUCATION
(internal and external)
Framing the system as valuable
nonprofit community partner

INTERNAL PARTNERSHIPS
COE/executive/board
Physician
Administrative
Departmental

MEETING DONOR NEEDS
Funding interests
Communications
Involvement

COMMUNICATIONS
Broad
Strategic
Purposive

PHILANTHROPY INVESTMENT
Resources devoted to fundraising activity
Major and planned giving focus

EXTERNAL PARTNERSHIPS
Mission
Focus on communities of need

Well-Established

High Fundraising
Performance

Culture of Philanthropy

one-time gifts. For investments to be continued, fundraising resources must be devoted to cultivating new relationships.

What performance benchmarking enables is a better understanding of lucrative fundraising activities. It delivers measurement that operating managers understand. Furthermore, it allows fundraisers to allocate resources into productive fundraising business lines and adjust according to a changing environment, all while enabling them to achieve closure on objectives monthly. Moreover, it stresses the interdependence of the many environmental and operating factors inherent in our hospital or health care system that are important to philanthropic success.

The real management value and true benefit of performance benchmarking are that they will identify best practices within business lines and offer measurement tools to assess and adjust activity that achieves annual and longer-term goals. Early indications from the collaborative work point to seven performance indicators present in higher-performing organizations. They are reflected in Figure 9.1.

STUART R. SMITH *is president and chief executive officer for Banner Health Foundation in Phoenix, Arizona.*

Philanthropic leadership is being challenged to lead change and elevate the status and value of health care philanthropy.

10

Identifying points of conflict

Terry Upshaw Morgan

We have met the enemy and it is us.
Pogo, by Walt Kelly

SEASONED HEALTH CARE philanthropic executives are rapidly becoming key to issues facing health care. Through the delivery of significant income, at the lowest possible cost, while providing a multitude of other services to promote, collaborate, and develop new business and high-level relationships, philanthropy is adding significant benefit to the organization and community. The opportunity is clear, but who is leading as an agent of change?

Pogo, the opossum protagonist in one of America's best-loved comic strips, summed it up for us. Even a 'possum could see that the root of human conflict is almost invariably human beings.

To overcome current points of conflict affecting health care philanthropy, our constituencies—donors as well as boards, administrative leadership, health care personnel, physicians, patients, vendors, volunteers, the community at large, and legislators—must understand the current health care environment. Furthermore, constituents need to understand key components integral to a successful fundraising program and the opportunities that surface when woven into the overall health system strategic plan. Only

NEW DIRECTIONS FOR PHILANTHROPIC FUNDRAISING, NO. 49, FALL 2005 © WILEY PERIODICALS, INC.

then will the synergy and true value of philanthropy be understood.

There is much to accomplish and strong evidence to support the need for a seat at the executive roundtable if philanthropy is to be a part of the solution. This chapter covers current points of conflict as they relate to health care philanthropy. It challenges philanthropic leadership to lead the change and provide opportunities to benefit health care organizations in a more meaningful way while increasing the value of philanthropy.

Conflict area 1: Is it underappreciation of philanthropy's contribution or our efforts to lead the change?

To understand that question, we must explore the issues surrounding return on investment in health care fundraising, executive leadership, and executive compensation.

Recognition of the return on investment

Some health care CEOs and their boards are waking up to the idea that beyond slim to no hospital margin, there is hope in the form of philanthropy. Funding of universities and the arts, to mention just two philanthropic sectors, has long been dependent on philanthropy for survival.

Traditionally there are two ways health care organizations enhance their financial ability: (1) developing their bottom line through operations and the development of new, competitive products and services or (2) borrowing through a number of banking or bond-related initiatives that pledge or leverage the company's assets. (See Chapter Two, this volume.)

Today, philanthropy takes its place at the table to complete the financing triad. This third leg, if you will, provides financial stability or balance to an otherwise healthy operations budget. When referring to this concept, one enlightened CFO reportedly said that it is as if we have discovered the financial holy grail.

For some, it is a final option that keeps the mission alive during difficult times. For others, it means providing the extra capital, education, research, and community benefit that goes beyond what budgets provide in service to the community. "The continuing constraints on health care reimbursement will accentuate the key role for philanthropy in the future. Philanthropy will be an increasingly critical factor in a health care organization's ability to access the capital resources necessary to meet the needs of its community," said Dale Collins, president and CEO of Baptist Health System of East Tennessee.

A place at the table

Foundation executives and chief development officers (CDOs) need to be driving this conversation at the top, working with the CEO and trustees to inform, plan, and commit. As a member of the executive council or roundtable, the CDO has the opportunity to listen, strategize, serve, and benefit the organization in new and meaningful ways. Just as the chief operating officer (COO) and chief financial officer (CFO) have ultimate system responsibility for hospital operations and finance, respectively, the foundation executive or CDO is responsible for system or hospital philanthropy.

This means responsibility for a board composed of CEOs, physicians, business leaders, philanthropists, and other community leaders who have the ability not only to give and get, but to lead others to the organization. Think in terms of traditional business development and the opportunity to drive business (patients) through insurance products or to health care programs and services.

While mission, vision, values, strategies, and health care goals are a given, core business lines are very different. Operational and financial management and measurements vary widely, as do community benefit and volunteer management (a thousand or more unpaid community staff). Add to this the stewardship functions of a foundation or development office, and you have an entirely different form of technical, research, and financial needs.

Executive compensation

Truly great leadership is increasingly hard to find. While responsibility and performance have increased, salaries have been slow to measure up to others at the executive health care level. In many cases, the senior foundation executive is managing a large board and subcommittees, numerous councils and ancillary committees, thousands of volunteers, and the foundation and development staff. They are responsible for managing all elements of fundraising annual and long-term programs, funds management, financial management inclusive of money management, general stewardship, board and staff education, and public relations and marketing for foundation and development in good times and crisis management during times of negative press. They are to establish the philanthropic culture and strategy both internally and externally.

In addition, most officers are responsible for community benefit, social accountability, and mini grants. They are typically sharing their leadership ability with many other civic projects to benefit the community as well. Arguably, there is justification as to why this is a demanding job and interesting that there is great overlap in skill sets as they relate to CEO, COO, or other senior vice president business development functions in the same or other more lucrative field.

The CDO is responsible for putting a healthy sum to the bottom line, often with less staff, technology, and consulting support. As value changes, so too will the compensation.

Salary benchmarks

While the CEO and board compensation committee rely on salary benchmarks for annual evaluation, when it comes to health care philanthropy, there are not many new data available. Typically a human resource vice president gathers salary reports for senior positions through their traditional sources. Several examples are the Hospital Association by state and region surveys, the Hay Group Hospital Compensation Survey, and the Watson Wyatt Hospital and Health Care Compensation Report. When it comes to philanthropic leadership, it is harder to find good data.

Using current market intelligence, nationally known headhunters are reporting significant differences in salaries. What is increasingly apparent is that successful foundation and development executives are commanding higher compensation than in the past. "Today's philanthropic executive is commanding a much higher compensation package. We are seeing a major increase in base rate pay and bonus opportunity," reports Curt Lucas, senior client partner at Korn/Ferry International. "It's a matter of depth of need, community competition, and past performance. Our pool of resources is shrinking; thus, great candidates with successful records of accomplishment are starting to see compensation more in line with other health care executives. In the old days, it was more about maintaining the status quo, versus aggressively growing, expanding, and contributing to the bottom line of the organization through foundation efforts."

Conflict area 2: Misunderstanding of philanthropy's role

Questions arise as to whether our constituencies understand the need for health care philanthropy. The development office has many messages to convey, including the difference between for-profit and nonprofit hospitals, community benefit, and rising health care costs.

Constituencies: Do they get it?

There are many components to philanthropy, and it is certainly more than just great events and free publicity. Figure 10.1 is a standard chart of business programs for most foundations and development offices inclusive of community benefit.

It is not just the frills

In the good old days of healthy profits and reserves, when philanthropy was not essential to most and some nonprofits were making so much money one would have to question the definition of *nonprofit*, foundations and development offices provided frills and in most cases managed public relations and marketing for their organizations as well. Foundation development officers were considered by some as the "party arm" of the organization. After all, they knew how to throw a great party, generated the right crowd, and secured free publicity.

Securing free publicity is still true today, but most foundations and development offices are needed to offset the bottom line, yet

Figure 10.1. Programs for community benefit

Income Programs		Stewardship Programs	
Annual Giving	**Deferred Giving**	**Organizational**	**Community Benefit**
• Annual Giving Club/Circles	• Wills	• Board Development	• Council
• Employee Drive	• Planned Gifts	• Nominating	• Goals
• Physician Drive	• Trusts	• Long Range Planning	• Mini Grants
• Memorial/Gifts to Honor	• Property Gifts	• Finance & Investment	• Collaborations
• Special Events	• Advisor Council	• Fundraising Consulting	• Clinics
• Grateful Patients	• Community Forums	• Donor Recognition	• Data Collection
• Campaign		• Donor Acquisition	• Accountability
• Major Gifts		• Communications/Newsletter	
• Internet		• Internet	
• Direct Mail		• Donor Management	
		• PR/Marketing	

their constituencies do not understand why this is necessary. Educating constituencies is key. In addition to traditional case statement development, it is critical that we focus on developing an understanding around issues facing health care financing. (See Chapters Two and Six, this volume.)

A recent survey conducted by the Advisory Board Company (2004) in discussion with participating CDOs cited concerns around the next decade of funding available for health care resources, questions around how hospitals will capitalize their future, and issues around losing charitable status and implications for philanthropy.

Beyond this, constituencies need to understand that in order to have the opportunity for new capital, cutting-edge technology, replacement facilities to handle the natural aging of many health care facilities, educational dollars to help offset the nursing shortage, research, funding, and supplies for community benefit, philanthropy or borrowing is required. We cannot count on investments to make us whole. The Advisory Board Company cites an unprecedented hospital need for capital in the decade ahead, as shown in Figures 10.2 and 10.3.

Figure 10.2. Percentage of inpatient procedures using devices

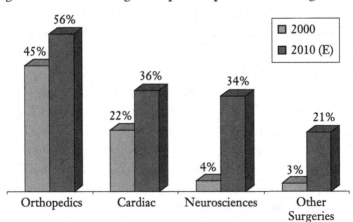

Source: Advisory Board Company (2003, p. 3).

Figure 10.3. U.S. hospital inpatient days, 2000–2010

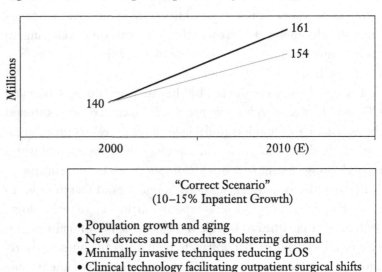

Source: Advisory Board Company (2003, p. 3).

Community benefit: At the heart, nonprofit versus for profit

One of the roles that the foundation can help a health care system fulfill and communicate is community benefit. As health care dollars grow thin, the foundation is in a unique position to identify needs, encourage collaborations, and communicate how the health system is helping to address these needs.

Health care continues to change, and the nonprofit status of hospitals is being challenged to prove their benefit. (See Chapter Eleven, this volume.) We need to encourage and participate in the development of standard criteria and measurement tools for defining community benefit. There is a need to be proactive and show leadership in discussions about benchmarking. We need to participate in educating the community as a whole about health care financing, nonprofit status, and what it means to give back.

The hospital is in trouble, and it is budget-cutting time

The very idea that someone would give $1 million in exchange for goodwill does not compute. Thus, spending money to cultivate donors may seem wasteful. This is particularly true when a health system is struggling to stay whole and every product line is being scrubbed for reductions. Rather than looking at return on the dollar, more often than not it is the old mentality of "one for all and all for one" across all entities.

When there are productivity issues at the hospital and personnel cuts to be made, executives should be wary. Foundations are not hospitals, and therefore must not be managed like them.

Document your performance; show the return on investment and cost to put dollars on the bottom line before agreeing to the cuts. This is one of the few good opportunities for new income and cash flow at low cost and should be championed by the CDO and board.

Conflict area 3: The need for coordination and communication with our constituency

It is important to have the facts straight. Our constituencies must be made aware of what makes managing a nonprofit health care institution different from managing a for-profit corporation.

Malaise

Constituencies do not understand why health care organizations, with such sophisticated budget and forecasting practices, monitoring software, pricey billings, and expensive consultants, are not capable of managing the bottom line. To corporate America, it must seem absurd.

Have your facts straight around case mix, patient days, staffing and productivity, Medicare and Medicaid reimbursement, and insurance-driven medicine. Relate the high cost of indigent care, and be prepared to share the amount of community benefit provided.

Compare that to the tax liability if you were a for-profit organization. There is usually a very wide gap between the two that demonstrates the additional burden being shouldered by nonprofit organizations. Finally, remind donors how expensive it is to bring new technology to the community, offset nursing shortages and agency nursing, and provide needed patient and staff education.

From one-on-one communication to a variety of traditional methods (direct mail, advertising, special reports, newsletters, e-mail, web design, and on-site presentations with physicians, board member, or CEO in tow), it is paramount we focus on a dialogue with our donors, board, and legislators. They must understand our case. They need to have a clear understanding of key issues affecting health care, why the margins may be slim to none, and why their support of philanthropy is important to our future.

Invigorating board-constituency communication

Access to information regarding plans for the future and new health care and infrastructure technology, capital needs, research, community benefit and epidemiological opportunities, nursing and other personnel needs, physician needs, education, vendor needs, and, most important, patient needs and real success stories are key to conversations with our constituencies. It is equally important that we communicate our nonprofit status and share our financial position and concerns. Informed and inspired constituents make their support decisions based on this information.

Budget forecasting and expectations

Most CFOs and health care finance departments do not understand philanthropy—its programs or the philosophies and business practices behind it. To compensate for the lack of system and accounting support in this area, foundations and development offices must develop their own template for budget planning; after the process is complete, they must summarize the budget into line items approved and used by a health care organization. The criteria in play revolve around the ability to roll up foundation budget information in the overall master budget.

It is like putting a round peg in a square hole. Forcing the information into three, four, or five line item slots has no bearing on foundation or development programs. This culminates in reporting that does not show program performance or other details important to monitoring performance. It is incumbent on foundation and development leadership to communicate with accounting and work to provide an understanding of what is needed to move and manage programs efficiently.

Silo mentality: Who are you going to call?

In most cases, philanthropy is not integrated in foundation, public relations, marketing, sales, managed care and insurance, and business development functions. There is much to be gained for all through the adoption of a communication plan that includes routine meetings between these departments.

Foundation accounting versus hospital accounting

It is important to know when the cash flow slows. Given the nuances of financial challenge to many organizations, you may be caught without a policy and procedure for paying foundation obligations. Again, it is a separate business with obligations unlike the hospital at large. You need to be informed immediately if your bills are not being paid and if donor distributions (the purpose for which you were given funding) are not taking place as directed.

Furthermore, it is important to communicate with donors, particularly vendor donors, who are not being paid for 60, 90, or 120 days. In the best of circumstances, you can work around it and save a donor relationship. In the worst of situations, the donor is lost and tells everyone he or she knows about the situation, which may lead to negative press and more. It is wise to stay ahead of this.

Health Insurance Portability and Accountability Act challenges

The Health Insurance Portability and Accountability Act (HIPAA) has forced us to spend more money to acquire new donors and much more time on the process to develop a successful direct mail program. Before HIPAA, patient information was provided to the foundation and included the diagnosis-related group. When mailing, you knew from the start that your prospect had a connection and perhaps interest in the subject matter. Today direct mail and donor acquisition programs must use the shotgun approach, which means mailing to a list of patients without benefit of connection to solicitation need. This results in excess postage, printing materials, labor, and other costs. Duplicate this by all health-related nonprofits trying to secure funding from patients who may want to participate, and you have millions of dollars in new cost to health care fundraising that could have been directed to patient care or new capital.

Along those same lines, one of the more lucrative forms of fundraising today is working directly with a lead physician who understands the cash flow constraints and wants to be more proactive in raising funds to secure new capital for the benefit of their particular specialty. HIPAA regulations require care to ensure patient confidentiality.

Outdated technology

New enabling information technology (IT) solutions, which can deliver an attractive return on investment when implemented as part of an overall strategy, will figure prominently in this endeavor. For example, shrinking margins make it impossible for the some systems to stay current with emerging computer hardware and software and communications technology. Philanthropy and various programs rely on sophisticated software programs that when upgraded do not run on old computer technology. Decisions around financial investment versus opportunity exist. Research, data, template, record keeping, reporting, and design needs are changing, as does the technology to support these areas. Our ability to create needed invitations, programs, donor recognition, and PowerPoint presentations are often developed by foundation staff and downloaded from the Internet. Aggressive IS leadership in an effort to employ the "one for all, all for one" mentality renders technology useless in an effort to maintain a level playing field throughout the house. Again, it is a different business requiring different treatment.

Benchmarking and best practices

Now that philanthropy is effectively adding to the health care equation, there is a greater need to validate productivity. A tool used by many is the Association for Healthcare Philanthropy (AHP) *USA Report on Giving.* Now in its twentieth series, it serves as a tracking tool for funds raised and fundraising expenditures, and it benchmarks a variety of useful and relevant programmatic factors.

Measurements and benchmarks for many categories in the report include funds raised by source, type of donor, and type of fundraising activity, along with expenditures by type of fundraising activity, planned giving by type and expense, allocations of time by fundraising activity, source of fundraising program expenses, use and distribution of funds raised, funds raised per dollar expended by type of institution, funds raised per dollar by staff size (full time), funds raised per dollar by fundraising expenses, and funds raised per dollar by bed size. This survey also compares data by institution type, geographical scope, and population.

However, of the 1,290 U.S. survey recipients who were e-mailed a link to the fiscal year 2003 survey instrument, only 260 returned useable surveys. There is so much change in this industry, and one of the most pressing issues is having good benchmarks, data, and best practices on which to bank.

AHP is creating learning circles to establish best practices. The first circle began its work in 2003, with the second circle beginning work in 2005. Each circle is made up of ten to twelve foundations from across the United States and Canada. Each circle is on a three-year cycle. The issues studied relate to items like cost per dollar raised, return on investment, donor conversion rates, performance per development officer, CEO participation, funds raised per full-time-equivalent employee by source, donor retention and renewal rates, board member participation, percentage funds raised by source, professional staff investment, and penetration of community giving.

Conclusion

Philanthropy represents the artful ability of matching knowledge of need with those for whom the capacity to give and passion for care help meet or exceed budget capacity in service to our community. It is incumbent on the foundation executive or CDO to educate the CEO of the system and all constituencies. It is time to push to embed philanthropic business programs in the strategic planning process for the benefit of our organizations and community.

Your challenge is to commit to lead the change. Address these issues head on. Be part of the solution. Push those silos to engage in philanthropy. Use your information to eliminate conflict. Lead in the effort to create new partnerships with those constituencies that may have been part of the conflict. Lest we forget, Pogo also said, "We are overwhelmed by insurmountable opportunity." The time is now. Lead the change!

References

Advisory Board Company. *Marketing and Planning Leadership Council Practice Brief.* Washington, D.C.: Advisory Board Company, 2003.

Advisory Board Company. *The Philanthropy 100—Elevating Philanthropy's Contribution to American Health Care.* Washington, D.C.: Advisory Board Company, 2004.

TERRY UPSHAW MORGAN *is senior vice president and executive director with Baptist Health System Foundation in Knoxville, Tennessee.*

With the recent scrutiny of hospital pricing and collections and hospital billing problems, it is imperative that development officers retain the public trust. What effective tactics and lessons can be learned from outside the hospital industry?

11

Sudden scrutiny of hospital billing and collections: Managing the oppositional crisis

Mary Anne Chern

RECENTLY DEVELOPMENT PROFESSIONALS have been dismayed by the sudden nationwide scrutiny of hospital pricing and collections, initially by the media and subsequently by legislative bodies, labor unions, and members of the public. There seems to be no fix in sight. Public perception is that the hospital industry is unwilling to correct the problem, at the same time that hospitals' charges skyrocket. With regard to the enhanced scrutiny, as one of my board members explained to me, "It goes to the basic issue of trust."

Philanthropy is a crucial component of providing state-of-the-art health care in this country. The Association for Health Care Philanthropy cited in its 2003 *Report on Giving* that total funds raised by all health care organizations in the United States reached almost $5.9 billion. Of these monies, 24.9 percent were designated for equipment, 18.3 percent for construction and renovation, and 13.0 percent for general operations. This funding is a crucial source

NEW DIRECTIONS FOR PHILANTHROPIC FUNDRAISING, NO. 49, FALL 2005 © WILEY PERIODICALS, INC.

of income for hospitals that makes it possible to fund construction, equipment, or programs the hospitals might not otherwise be able to afford.

Recent scrutiny by the media and government

Many key donors and volunteers are corporate CEOs who read the *Wall Street Journal*, just one of the major publications to focus on hospitals for their pricing methods, zealous collections practices, and spiraling health care costs. Many of the media stories feature testimonials of patients who have figured out that the same procedure or hospital stay may result in different charges to the patient depending on the patient's insurance status.

Lucette Lagnado's front-page story in the *Wall Street Journal*, "Forgoing Insurance, Mr. Selby Bargains for his Health Care," is subtitled "Shopping Around, He Finds Discounts on Treatments: Pay Upfront, Get 30% Off." Selby is self-employed and middle class, which means he does not meet the criteria for charity care established by hospital policies. (Most hospitals have an indigent discount payment program, referred to as a charity care policy.) Selby's story is compelling. When he was diagnosed with prostate cancer, he was told by University of California-San Francisco (UCSF) that treatment would cost approximately $80,000 to $100,000. Because Selby was uninsured, his cost of health care was not reduced by the discounts commonly negotiated by health maintenance organizations and insurance carriers. He then checked with Loma Linda University Medical Center, which initially quoted him $80,000 but this price was negotiated down to between $36,000 and $38,000. Going back to UCSF, Selby reached an agreement whereby the hospital would ask him to pay only $25,000. The hospital covered the remainder of its list price of $88,652 by taking $34,000 from a private philanthropic fund maintained at the hospital, and the hospital wrote off the rest as charity care. Lagnado goes on to criticize hospitals for making it so difficult for consumers to determine pricing. Karen Davis, president of the Commonwealth Fund, a private foundation in New York that focuses on health care policy, criticizes the pricing system by saying, "When your child is injured, do you call and say, 'Now, which orthopedist will fix this collarbone the cheapest?'" (Lagnado, 2004, p. 2).

The public questioning of patient billing processes has renewed interest in the tax-exempt status of hospitals, from which local, state, and federal authorities have sought to secure new tax revenue. (Federal law exempts nonprofits from income tax and allows tax deductions for gifts to such organizations; state law provides exemption from sales and property taxes. Nor do hospitals pay estate taxes, since the tax is imposed on estates and not organizations.)

The reasoning behind tax exemption is that nonprofit organizations invest in the community by serving as a safety net: caring for those unable to pay and providing other community benefit services through venues such as low-cost health screenings, free transportation, and educational programs. In 2004 the U.S. House Ways and Means Committee announced it would be investigating whether nonprofits are behaving too much like for-profits, and local authorities in at least three states launched cases challenging the tax-exempt status of nonprofit hospitals (Taylor, 2004a).

Dichotomy between nonprofit and for-profit

In many ways the nonprofit hospital industry and their administrations have exacerbated the identity problem between for-profit and nonprofit. They have failed to distinguish their nonprofit hospital as a charity in the public's mind. Hospital administration benefits from salary surveys that typically separate hospitals based on number of beds and number of employees, with bigger size equating to larger salaries and status. Charity work in the community and philanthropy are not as valued as operations, as evidenced by management teams that shortsightedly exclude the senior development officer. While corporate positioning works for big business, nonprofit hospitals need to refocus on their social mission. College presidents have been highly successful in raising money for their schools by focusing on their investment in the students and the community; nonprofit hospitals and their leaders would be better served by modeling the college president and the education model, as opposed to corporate America.

First and foremost, a nonprofit hospital and its leaders must focus on mission. In our role as fundraisers, it is our responsibility to ensure that our nonprofit tax status is well deserved. We need to help the administration position the institution in the community so as to ensure our tax-exempt status is not questioned.

Lawsuits and congressional oversight generate concern

Mississippi plaintiff attorney Richard Scruggs and other class action attorneys, who successfully sued the tobacco and asbestos industries, filed lawsuits against hospitals in fifteen states in summer 2004. Mark Taylor's legal update in *Modern Health Care* reports that "Scruggs and his clients allege that the named hospitals violated their tax-exempt status by overcharging and discriminating in their billing practices against poor and uninsured patients . . . and committed a breach of contract, consumer fraud, unjust enrichment, deceptive billing practices and conspiracy" (Taylor, 2004b, p. 14). Scruggs stated that he intends to show that "'hospitals have for years spent only a small percentage of their sizable revenues on charity care for the uninsured while reaping enormous windfalls from their tax-exempt status, according to Taylor'" (Taylor, 2004b, p. 14). The attorneys for the plaintiffs further allege that hospitals are "'hoarding billions while dispensing pennies'" (Clarke, 2004, p. 40).

While the AHA responded that the Scruggs lawsuits are without merit, the notoriety from the case is sure to have an impact on an already concerned public regardless of the outcome.

Stephen Weyl, an attorney, reported to Jaklevic of *Modern Health Care* that his firm and Health Capital Group, a valuation firm, are now requiring hospital clients needing to borrow money to include an assessment of their charity care in bond prospectuses because "investors want to make sure there is no risk that a hospital could lose its tax exemption, which would create tax liabilities and dampen charitable contributions, or incur patient lawsuits" (Jaklevic, 2004, p. 7).

At the same time three congressional committees launched investigations into the billing policies and charity care at hospitals, with special focus on the nonprofit sector (Tieman and Fong, 2004).

Labor unions and consumer advocates target hospitals

While providers continue to say they are doing their best to serve uninsured and underinsured patients, labor unions and consumer advocates have targeted the industry's perceived weaknesses.

In a special report for *Modern Health Care*, Melanie Evans notes that the Service Employees International Union (SEIU) has launched the Hospital Accountability Project. She quotes Joseph Geevarghese, who is leading the project for the SEIU, who claims, "'Ours is a movement for social and economic justice'" (Evans, 2004, p. 26). Consumer advocates and members of the clergy have been enlisted to help the effort. The SEIU's Web site discussed hospital pricing and collections, with special focus on patient testimonials about billing practices. Labor experts see a large SEIU war chest and claim the activity is a thinly disguised corporate campaign to increase membership and dues to the unions, given that support for unions has waned (albeit slightly) in recent years. Among health care professionals and medical technicians, union membership dropped from 12.5 percent of workforce share in 2002 to 12.3 percent in 2003 (Evans, 2004).

The facts about charity care

It is a common mistake to think that IRS law requires charity care. Current IRS law actually only requires a nonprofit hospital to operate an emergency room available to all patients regardless of whether they can pay. Of course, since many indigent patients use the emergency room as an urgent care center and the majority of patient admissions are generated by the emergency room, many indigent patients treated in the emergency room end up being admitted.

Despite an IRS directive to include charitable services on Form 990, many hospitals still fail to report their charity care publicly. More and more grant-making foundations and savvy donors are using GuideStar to look at these forms. A recent survey on GuideStar by *Modern Healthcare* of twenty-one hospitals showed more than half listed no charity care data, which is really a lost opportunity (Jaklevic, 2004).

Making the subject of charity care reporting even more confusing is the fact that there have not been nationally accepted guidelines for reporting charity care, and some hospitals report the actual cost of providing care while others report the full price. Jakelvic notes that "further clouding the issue, often no distinction is drawn between charity care, which is provided without expectation of payment, and bad debt, in which charges are billed and not paid. In reporting community benefits, some hospitals lump in shortfalls generated by services to Medicaid and Medicare patients, volunteers' time, medical education costs, discounts to third-party payers and the costs of operating health fairs and screenings" (Jaklevic 2004, p. 7). This lack of accountability and transparency within the industry erodes public confidence and trust.

History of the pricing and collections problem

The billing system for hospitals evolved over years, as opposed to being created out of whole cloth. The result, and as mandated by Medicare, is a comprehensive price list for services provided, known as a charge master. Some hospitals have charge masters listing over forty thousand separate charges. The result is a billing system that, especially for the layperson, is as difficult to understand as the IRS tax code.

Increased charges and reduced reimbursement

In 2002 health spending grew at a rate of 9.3 percent, according to a report by the Commonwealth Fund (Collins and others, 2004). Two in five adult (41 percent) Americans say they are having difficulty paying their medical bills, and 27 percent report they have to forgo food, heat, or rent in order to make payments toward their medical bills, according to the same Commonwealth Fund report. This was the greatest annual increase in a decade in the world's most expensive health care system (Blendon and others, 2003). The shame of the American health care system is that despite these expenditures, Americans still do not have the best health among developed nations, as Blandon points out. Nor has it reduced the number of uninsured, which recently climbed to 45 million nationwide (Tieman, 2004). Almost double that number lacked health insurance at some time during the year, and many more are underinsured, according to David Bernd, chair of the AHA's board of trustees (Bernd, 2004).

Blue Cross and Blue Shield have been quick to blame hospitals for health care increases, noting in 2004 that "hospitals are the largest component of health care expenditures, accounting for over half of private insurers' spending growth" (Benko, 2004b, p. 16). The average cost of a hospital admission jumped 11 percent from 2000 to 2002, costing $7,353 (Benko, 2004b). The AHA has vigorously disputed the charge by the insurers, noting that hospital overall operating margins declined from 3.7 percent in 2002 to 3.3 percent in 2003, at a time when insurers experienced record profit margins (Benko, 2004b).

Some experts attribute part of the cost increases to ballooning technology. There were 300 million MRI scans performed nationally in 2001, and this number is projected to increase to 500 million in 2008 (Benko, 2004b). Since the number of X rays is not declining, this is just one example of added cost generated by better technology.

Other experts place the blame on reduced reimbursement, especially the uninsured and underinsured. According to David Bernd and the AHA, in 2002 hospitals absorbed over $22 billion in costs for providing uncompensated care to patients (Bernd, 2004). The high penetration of managed care in many markets has also reduced hospital reimbursement. And labor and liability costs continue to rise. Still other experts cite burgeoning administrative costs, exacerbated by confusing regulations and legal challenges. In sum, a recent Centers for Medicare and Medicaid Services study shows that in 2002, hospitals drove health care spending, accounting for thirty cents spent from every health care dollar in this country ("Health Care Spending Reaches $1.6 Trillion in 2002," 2004).

The truth, of course, is that all these factors play a crucial role in increasing charges and reducing reimbursement.

The AHA and individual hospitals respond to scrutiny

The AHA responded to the increased scrutiny of hospital pricing and collections by publishing the following Principles and Guidelines in December 2003 (Bernd, 2004, p. 2):

1. Treat all patients equitably, with dignity, with respect and with compassion.
2. Serve the emergency health care needs of everyone, regardless of a patient's ability to pay for care.
3. Assist patients who cannot pay for part or all of the care they receive.
4. Balance needed financial assistance for some patients with broader fiscal responsibilities in order to keep hospitals' doors open for all who may need care.

The AHA has taken a proactive approach to the controversy surrounding patient billing and is now providing prototype policies and procedures to address billing issues and charity care to members. It has also called on the federal government for increased transparency in the billing system.

In California, the California Health Care Association has developed a helpful checklist for hospitals revising or developing a charity care policy. But even hospital supporters note that more is needed. Todd Sloane, the assistant managing editor/op-ed for *Modern Health Care*, notes that "a lack of clarity of mission and poor reporting by many in the industry invited this deluge of scrutiny" and criticizes nonprofit hospitals and systems that act like for-profits while ignoring their charitable mission. He calls for the hospital industry to "clarify and promulgate its charitable activities, sharply discount bills for the uninsured and adopt patient-friendly billing" (Sloane, 2004, p. 17).

To date, the AHA has resisted public disclosure of charge masters. In a congressional hearing, the AHA's chair cited the difficulty the public would have with the extensive list of charges and instead proposed other meaningful ways in which to disseminate charge information (Bernd, 2004). The Health Care Financial Management Association, in partnership with the AHA and others, has launched the Patient Friendly Billing Project to improve financial communication between hospitals and patients (Clarke, 2004).

In the meantime, policymakers continue their scrutiny of hospitals' charity care policies and billing systems. A bill introduced in the California legislature would make that state the first to cap what the uninsured can be charged. Benko notes that "hospitals also would be required to file charity-care reports with the state, post their reduced-fee policies in admitting areas and emergency rooms, inform patients of their financial assistance options, including payment plans, and wait at least 150 days before trying to collect any unpaid bills from uninsured patients" (Benko, 2004a, p. 7).

Managing the challenge at the hospital level

At White Memorial Medical Center, we addressed the overall issue of charity care and investment in the community by creating a strategic action team with members from various departments: patient billing, administration, finance, government relations, public relations, marketing, business development, and fundraising. Unlike an episodic crisis—a single event like the Tylenol poisonings—our task has been to develop a plan to deal with oppositional crisis, in which opposition is both organized and sustainable.

One emphasis has been to develop a public information program. Our first focus has been on educating our boards and key volunteers about the issues, and especially explaining to them our charity care policy. Our information sharing has included handouts, presentations, and question-and-answer sheets. Any good crisis management plan notes the importance of identifying neutral third parties who are perceived as fair and neutral. By educating our foundation board members, who are well respected and have high visibility in the community, we have laid the groundwork for dealing with any specific attacks targeting our hospital. As part of our public information program, we have also developed testimonials by patients who have benefited from the charity care policy. The public relations team has also developed internal strategies for educating staff and physicians. And all presentations emphasize that the hospital endorses the AHA policy and guidelines.

The hospital is also focusing on sharing the good works it does in the community. In California, all nonprofit hospitals are required to conduct a community needs assessment, as well as document to the state an annual community benefits plan—for example, how the hospital will help meet community needs. For the past several years, we have included the year-end results of the previous year's community benefits plan on our IRS 990s.

Another key area of emphasis has been our elected officials. We have provided them with educational materials. Our hospital has also encouraged public officials to hold press conferences about health care issues at our facility. We want the public to know that we are working in concert with elected officials.

We have also begun to focus on the economic benefits our hospital brings to the community, at the suggestion of one of our key volunteers, a banker. To date, we have emphasized dollars spent on local businesses, numbers of hospital employees who live in the hospital's service area, and number of persons employed by our new construction.

Research hospitals have an additional opportunity to tout their social benefit value. Improved health and increased life span equates to productivity, and "according to Delos Cosgrove, M.D., CEO of The Cleveland Clinic, more than $57 trillion have been added to the U.S. economy through extended life spans" (Beckham, 2004, p. 2). Johns Hopkins University (which includes Johns Hopkins Medical) contributed $7 billion to the Maryland economy in 2002 in direct and indirect spending, more than double that in 1990 (Beckham, 2004). While a corporation's value is set by shareholder value, both social and economic impact must be considered to determine the true value of a hospital to its community. Unlike the proverbial company that makes widgets, where value is based on the number of widgets made, hospitals invest in their communities; only by assessing all elements of that investment (jobs created, and that people are healthy enough to work and care for children, for example) can a hospital's value be determined.

In addition to the public relations aspect, it is crucial to ensure that hospital billing focuses on customer service and making bills easy to understand. Greenwich Hospital in Connecticut began its initiative to overhaul its patient billing process almost ten years ago. The Patient Financial Office put together a task force of information systems staff, former patients from the community, physicians, billing personnel, and clinical employees. This team reviewed billing processes and made a number of significant changes to enhance customer service and reduce complaints. Cheryl Farrey, director of patient financial services, says that changes included customer service training for billing staff, dedicated time every day for staff to handle patient inquiries, and setting up a voice mail phone line for patients requesting more specific detail on charges. Another innovation was the creation of customized letters that are sent to patients, explaining what they should expect. The task force redesigned the patient invoice (the patient financial office has tried to eliminate confusion over the word *bill,* which may or may not be asking for payment). The invoice for payment outlines adjustments and insurance agreements, explaining how that reduces the overall amount due. Communication from the billing office also became friendlier and incorporated the phrase, "Thank you for using Greenwich Hospital. It was our privilege to serve you." Finally, the timing of the revenue cycle was changed so that patients were not billed until after insurance companies had made payment.

The outpatient billing process also received special focus at Greenwich Hospital. Outpatients are sent a detail of services, which has greatly contributed to satisfaction and reduced the number of questions received about services rendered. A customized letter sent to lab patients, who may or may not have been to the hospital, explains that "your physician sent us your lab specimen," which is why the patient is being billed by Greenwich Hospital.

To ensure accountability for customer satisfaction, each department director at Greenwich Hospital attends a weekly meeting chaired by the hospital CEO. All patient complaints are shared publicly at this weekly meeting. The department director must explain how the problem has been resolved and must also respond to the patient by calling that person and sharing what new process has been implemented. Even if the problem cannot be resolved, the patient is at least made aware that his concerns have been heard and discussed at the highest level of the organization, which has significantly added to patient satisfaction. The patient finance office also has key indicators it must meet on a weekly basis; these indicators include the length of time callers are placed on hold and the number of missed calls (that go to voice mail) on a weekly basis.

Conclusion

The intense scrutiny of hospital billing and collections is not going to go away. Careful management of public relations, staff and volunteer readiness to address charity care and tax exemption issues, and ongoing process improvements to ensure customer satisfaction within the hospital are essential. Recently Gary Hubbell (2004) warned of an upcoming decline in philanthropy and said that of necessity, "hospital development offices and CEOs will need to adopt a new stance, raise a new vision, and collaborate with new partners in order to be seen and accepted by donors as being part of the health care solution for society." The fundraiser can and should play the lead role steering his organization through this social change.

References

Association for Healthcare Philanthropy Canada & USA. *FY 2003 Report on Giving*. Falls Church, Va.: Association for Healthcare Philanthropy.

Beckham, D. "Economic Powerhouses in Medicine, Part 1." Beckham Company, 2004.

Benko, L. B. "Even-Steven." *Modern Healthcare*, Aug. 30, 2004a, 7–16.

Benko, L. B. "Passing the Buck." *Modern Healthcare*, Dec. 13, 2004b, 8–16.

Bernd, D. "Tax Exemption: Pricing Practices of Hospitals." Testimony of the American Hospital Association Before the U.S. House of Representatives Subcommittee on Oversight of the Committee on Ways and Means, June 22, 2004.

Blendon, R. J., and others. "Common Concerns amid Diverse Systems: Health Care Experiences in Five Countries." *Health Affairs*, 2003, *22*(3), 106–121.

Clarke, R. "Patient-Friendly Billing—the Sequel." *Modern Healthcare*, June 28, 2004, p. 40.

Collins, S. R., and others. *The Affordability Crisis in U.S. Health Care: Findings from the Commonwealth Fund Biennial Health Insurance Survey.* New York: Commonwealth Fund, 2004.

Evans, M. "Labor Pains." *Modern Healthcare*, Dec. 6, 2004, pp. 26–28.

"Health Care Spending Reaches $1.6 Trillion in 2002." *CMS News*, Jan. 8, 2004, p. 1.

Hubbell, G. J. *Forces of Change: The Coming Challenges in Hospital Philanthropy.* Falls Church, Va.: Association for Healthcare Philanthropy, 2004.

Jaklevic, M. C. "Well-Kept Secret." *Modern Healthcare*, June 21, 2004, p. 7.

Lagnado, L. "Faith and Credit: Forgoing Insurance, Mr. Selby Bargains for His Health Care." *Wall Street Journal*, Nov. 24, 2004, p. A1.

Sloane, T. "Mission Unaccomplished." *Modern Healthcare*, July 5, 2004, p. 17.

Taylor, M. "Exemption Granted." *Modern Healthcare*, Mar. 15, 2004a, pp. 6–9.

Taylor, M. "Scruggs' Hospital Lawsuit Grows." *Modern Healthcare*, July 12, 2004b, p. 14.

Tieman, J. "Unsure About the Uninsured." *Modern Healthcare*, Aug. 30, 2004, pp. 6–16.

Tieman, J., and Fong, T. "Surviving the Heat." *Modern Healthcare*, June 28, 2004, p. 6.

MARY ANNE CHERN *is president of White Memorial Medical Center Charitable Foundation in Los Angeles.*

Index

Back Issue/Subscription Order Form

Copy or detach and send to:

Jossey-Bass, A Wiley Company, 989 Market Street, San Francisco CA 94103-1741

Call or fax toll-free: Phone 888-378-2537 6:30AM – 3PM PST; Fax 888-481-2665

Back Issues: Please send me the following issues at $29 each
(Important: please include series initials and issue number, such as PF22.)

_____

_____

_____

$ _____   Total for single issues

$ _____   SHIPPING CHARGES: SURFACE   Domestic   Canadian

	Domestic	Canadian
First Item	$5.00	$6.00
Each Add'l Item	$3.00	$1.50

For next-day and second-day delivery rates, call the number listed above.

Subscriptions: Please __start __renew my subscription to *New Directions for Philanthropic Fundraising* for the year 2_____ at the following rate:

U.S.	__Individual $109	__Institutional $228
Canada	__Individual $109	__Institutional $268
All Others	__Individual $133	__Institutional $302

**For more information about online subscriptions visit
www.interscience.wiley.com**

$ _____   Total single issues and subscriptions (Add appropriate sales tax for your state for single issue orders. No sales tax for U.S. subscriptions. Canadian residents, add GST for subscriptions and single issues.)

__Payment enclosed (U.S. check or money order only)
__VISA __MC __AmEx #_____ Exp. Date _____

Signature _____ Day Phone _____
__ Bill Me (U.S. institutional orders only. Purchase order required.)

Purchase order # _____
    Federal Tax ID13559302   **GST 89102 8052**

Name _____

Address _____

_____

Phone _____ E-mail _____

For more information about Jossey-Bass, visit our Web site at www.josseybass.com